—HOT DAMN,
WE'RE GOING TO BUST THIS THING

"This is a revolution. It started long before I came into it, and I may die before it's over, but we'll bust this thing and cut out this cancer. America will be as strong and beautiful as it should be, for black folks and white folks. We'll all be free then, free from a system that makes a man less than a man, that teaches hate and fear and ignorance.

"You didn't die a slave for nothing, Momma. You brought us up. You and all those Negro mothers who gave their kids the strength to go on, to take that thimble to the well while the whites were taking buckets. Those of us who weren't destroyed got stronger, got calluses on our souls. And now we're ready to change a system, a system where a white man can destroy a black man with a single word. Nigger.

"When we're through, Momma, there won't be any niggers any more."

Nigger

an autobiography

by **DICK GREGORY**

with **ROBERT LIPSYTE**

POCKET BOOKS

New York   London   Toronto   Sydney

POCKET BOOKS, a division of Simon & Schuster, Inc.
1230 Avenue of the Americas, New York, NY 10020

ISBN 13: 978-0-671-73560-9
ISBN 10:   0-671-73560-8

First Pocket Books paperback printing February 1986
30 29 28 27 26 25 24 23 22 21

POCKET and colophon are registered trademarks of
Simon & Schuster, Inc.

For information regarding special discounts for bulk purchases,
please contact Simon & Schuster Special Sales at
1-800-456-6798 or business@simonandschuster.com

Printed in the U.S.A.

Dear Momma—Wherever you are, if ever you hear the word "nigger" again, remember they are advertising my book.

Contents

Richard Claxton Gregory was born on Columbus Day, 1932. A welfare case. You've seen him on every street corner in America. You knew he had rhythm by the way he snapped his cloth while he shined your shoes. Happy little black boy, the way he grinned and picked your quarter out of the air. Then he ran off and bought himself a Twinkie Cupcake, a bottle of Pepsi-Cola, and a pocketful of caramels.

You didn't know that was his dinner. And you never followed him home.

Not Poor, Just Broke

I

It's a sad and beautiful feeling to walk home slow on Christmas Eve after you've been out hustling all day, shining shoes in the white taverns and going to the store for the neighbors and buying and stealing presents from the ten-cent store, and now it's dark and still along the street and your feet feel warm and sweaty inside your tennis sneakers even if the wind finds the holes in your mittens. The electric Santa Clauses wink at you from windows. You stop off at your best friend's house and look at his tree and give him a ball-point pen with his name on it. You reach into your shopping bag and give something to everybody there, even the ones you don't know. It doesn't matter that they don't have anything for you because it feels so good to be in a warm happy place where grownups are laughing. There are Daddies around. Your best friend's so happy and excited, standing there trying on all his new clothes. As you walk down the stairs you hear his mother say: "Boo, you forgot to say good-by to Richard, say good-by to Richard, Boo, and wish him a . . ."

Then you're out on the street again and some of the lights have gone out. You take the long way home, and Mister Ben, the grocer, says: "Merry Christmas, Richard," and you give him a present out of the shopping bag, and you smile at a wino and give him a nickel, and you even wave at Grimes, the mean cop. It's a good feeling. You don't want to get home too fast.

And then you hit North Taylor, your street, and something catches your eye and you lift your head up and it's there in your window. Can't believe it. You start running and the only thing in the whole world you're mad about is that you can't run fast enough. For the first

3

time in a long while the cracked orange door says: "Come on in, little man, you're home now," and there's a wreath and lights in the window and a tree in the kitchen near the coal closet and you hug your Momma, her face hot from the stove. Oh, Momma, I'm so glad you did it like this because ours is new, just for us, everybody else's tree been up all week long for other people to see, and, Momma, ours is up just for us. Momma, oh, Momma, you did it again.

My beautiful Momma smiled at me like Miss America, and my brothers and sisters danced around that little kitchen with the round wooden table and the orange-crate chairs.

"Go get the vanilla, Richard," said Momma, "Presley, peel some sweet potatoes. Go get the bread out the oven, Dolores. You get away from that duckling, Garland. Ronald, oh, Ronald, you be good now, stand over there with Pauline. Oh, Richard, my little man, did you see the ham Miz White from the Eat Shop sent by, and the bag of nuts from Mister Myers and the turkey from Miz King, and wouldn't you know, Mister Ben, he . . ."

"Hey, Momma, I know some rich people don't got this much, a ham, and a turkey, Momma. . . ."

"The Lord, He's always looking out for my boys, Richard, and this ain't all, the white folks'll be by here tomorrow to bring us more things."

Momma was so happy that Christmas, all the food folks brought us and Mister Ben giving us more credit, and Momma even talked the electric man into turning the lights on again.

"Hey, Momma, look here, got a present for Daddy. A cigarette lighter, Momma, there's even a place to scratch a name on it."

"What you scratch on it, Richard, Big Pres or Daddy?"

"Nothing, Momma. Might have to give Daddy's present to old Mister White from the Eat Shop again."

She turned away and when she turned back her eyes were wet. Then she smiled her Miss America smile and grabbed my shoulder. "Richard, my little man, if I show you something, you won't tell nobody, will you?"

"What is it, Momma?"

"I got something for you."

"Oh, Momma, you forgot, everything's under the tree."

"This is something special, just for you, Richard."

"Thanks, Momma, oh, thanks, how'd you know I wanted a wallet, Momma, a real wallet like men have?"

Momma always gave each of us something special like that, something personal that wasn't under the tree, something we weren't supposed to tell the other kids about. It always came out, though. Garland and I'd be fighting and one of us would say, "Momma likes me better than you, look what she gave me," and we both found out the other got a secret present, too.

But I loved that wallet. First thing I did was fill out the address card. If I got hit by a car someone would know who I am. Then I put my dollars in it, just like men do. Ran outside that night and got on a streetcar and pulled out my wallet and handed the conductor a dollar.

"Got anything smaller, boy?"

"Sure, Mister," I said and I pulled out my wallet again and took a dime out of the coin purse and snapped it shut and put the dollar back in the long pocket and closed the wallet and slipped it into my back pocket. Did the same thing on the way back home.

Did we eat that night! It seemed like all the days we went without food, no bread for the baloney and no baloney for the bread, all the times in the summer when there was no sugar for the Kool-Aid and no lemon for the lemonade and no ice at all were wiped away. Man, we're all right.

After dinner I went out the back door and looked at the sky and told God how nobody ever ate like we ate that night, macaroni and cheese and ham and turkey and the old duckling's cooking in the oven for tomorrow. There's even whiskey, Momma said, for people who come by. Thanks, God, Momma's so happy and even the rats and roaches didn't come out tonight and the wind isn't blowing through the cracks.

How'd you know I wanted a wallet, God? I wonder if

all the rich people who get mink coats and electric trains got that one little thing nobody knew they wanted. You know, God, I'm kinda glad you were born in a manger. I wonder, God, if they had let Mary in the first place she stopped at, would you have remembered tonight? Oh, God, I'm scared. I wish I could die right now with the feeling I have because I know Momma's going to make me mad and I'm going to make her mad, and me and Presley's gonna fight. . . .

"Richard, you get in here and put your coat on. Get in here or I'll whip you."

See what I mean, God, there she goes already and I'm not even cold, I'm all wrapped up in You.

"What's wrong, Richard? Why you look so strange?"

"You wouldn't understand, Momma."

"I would, Richard, you tell me."

"Well, I came out to pray, Momma, way out here so they wouldn't hear me and laugh at me and call me a sissy. God's a good God, ain't He, Momma?"

"Yes, Richard."

"Momma, if I tell you something, would you laugh at me, would you say I'm crazy, would you say I was lying? Momma?"

"What is it. Richard?"

"I heard Him talk to me, Momma."

She put her arm around my shoulders and pulled me against her. "He talks to people, Richard, some people that are real special and good like you. Do me a favor, Richard?"

"Sure, Momma."

"Next time you talk to Him, ask Him to send Daddy home."

"Let me stay up and look out the window with you, Momma."

"Everybody's in bed, Richard."

"All my life, Momma, I wanted to stay up with you on Christmas Eve and look out that window with you, Momma. I won't laugh at you."

"What you mean, Richard?"

"You're waiting on him, ain't you? I know, Momma, every Christmas Eve you take a bath and put on that perfume and those clothes from the rich white folks and get down there on your knees in front of that window looking for Daddy."

"Richard, you better get on to bed."

"I know, Momma, that whiskey ain't for people coming by, that's for Daddy."

"Richard, you go on to bed and when he gets here I'll wake you up."

"No, Momma, I want to sit up with you . . . Momma?"

"Yes, Richard?"

"I shoulda got a present for Mister White, 'cause I know Daddy's coming to get his this year."

There were a lot of things I wanted to tell Momma that night while we sat and waited for Daddy, while we prayed on our knees, and dozed and hugged each other against the cold and jumped up like jacks every time we heard a noise on the street. But I never did. Sometimes I think she knew anyway.

I wanted to say to her, Momma, you remember that day I came home and told you I was at Doctor Jackson's house? And how he liked me, Momma, and told me I'd be a good doctor? How he's going to help me learn to read, and how he told me when it gets too cold to study in my house I could come by his house? Remember that, Momma? It was a lie. I played all that day in a vacant lot.

I guess she knew. She never pressed me for names when I told her about all the people who liked me, all the people I created in my mind, people to help poor folks. I couldn't believe God had made a world and hadn't put none of those people in it.

I made up a schoolteacher that loved me, that taught me to read. A teacher that didn't put me in the idiot's seat or talk about you and your kind. She didn't yell at me when I came to school with my homework all wrinkled and damp. She understood when I told her it was

too cold to study in the kitchen so I did my homework
under the covers with a flashlight. Then I fell asleep.
And one of the other five kids in bed must have peed on
it.

I'd go out and sweat and make five dollars. And I'd
come home and say, Momma, Mister Green told me to
bring this to you. Told me he liked you. Told me he
wished he could raise his kids the way you're raising us.
That wasn't true, Momma.

Remember all those birthday parties I went to, Momma? Used to steal things from the ten-cent store and give
the best presents. I'd come home and tell you how we
played pillow kiss and post office and pin the tail on the
donkey and how everybody liked me? That was a lie,
Momma. One girl cried and ran away when she threw
the pillow and it hit me. She opened her eyes and saw
she was supposed to kiss me and she cried and ran away.

And on my birthday, Momma, when I came home
with that shopping bag full of presents and told you the
kids in my class loved me so much they all got me
things? That wasn't true. I stole all those little things
from the ten-cent store and wrapped them up and put
a different kid's name on each one.

"Oh, Richard, if he don't show up this time . . ."
"He's comin', Momma, it's like you said. He got
held up in traffic, the trains were full."
"You know, Richard, your Daddy's a cook, he
has to work on Christmas."
"He'll be here, Momma, you go put those clothes
back on."

Remember when those people came by and told you how
dirty we were, how they didn't want us playing with their
kids or coming into their houses? They said we smelled
so bad. I was six then, and Presley was almost eight.
You cried all night, Momma, and then you told us to
stay home until you could get us some new clothes. And
you went and hid all the clothes we had. Momma, it was
summertime and we couldn't just lay there, crying and

watching out the window at the kids play running ▮
and rip and run, and get called in for their naps, and g▮
called in for their dinners. And we looked all over fo▮
our clothes, down in the basement, in the coal closet,
under the stove, and we couldn't find them. And then
we went through your things, Momma, and put on the
dresses you never wore, the dresses the rich white folks
gave you. And then we went outside to play. The people
laughed at us when we went outside in your dresses,
pointed and slapped their legs. We never played so good
as we played that summer, with all those people watching
us. When we came off the porch those Negro doctors
and lawyers and teachers waiting to get into White's Eat
Shop across the street would nudge each other and turn
their heads. And when the streetcar stopped on the
corner, right in front of our house, the people would
lean out the windows and stare. Presley and I would
wave at them. We did it all that summer, and after a
while nobody bothered us. Everybody got to know that
the Gregory boys didn't have clothes so they wore their
mother's dresses. We just made sure we were home before you got there, Momma.

"How do I look, Richard?"

"You look okay, Momma."

"These are the best pair of shoes I got, Miz Wal-
lace gave me them, but they're summer shoes."

"What you mean, summer shoes? Those are the
black and white ones I like so much, the ones you
never wear. I didn't know they were summer shoes."

"You never see folks wear white shoes in the win-
tertime."

"People dye them, Momma. I'll dye them for
you so you can put them on and Daddy can see
you."

"Oh, Richard, there won't be time, they got to
dry."

"Don't worry, Momma, you burn the dye and it
dries right while you wear it."

dyed a lot of shoes, Momma, down on my hands and knees in the taverns, dyeing shoes and shining shoes. I never told you too much about the things I did and the things I saw. Momma, remember the time I came home with my teeth knocked in and my lip all cut? Told you I tripped downstairs. Momma, I got kicked. Right in the face.

It was Saturday afternoon, my big hustling day. I was ten, but I looked like I was seven. There were a lot of people in the tavern, drinking beer, and I was shining this white woman's shoes. They were white and brown shoes, summer shoes. The men sitting at the bar were laughing.

"Hey, Flo, gonna take the little monkey home with you, change your luck?"

She started laughing. "Maybe I will. Heard these little coons are hung like horses, I'm getting tired of you worms."

"Little monkey's got a tail, Flo, swing from limb to limb."

White and brown shoes. I didn't want to get the brown polish on the white part so I put my other hand on the back of the white woman's leg to steady myself.

"He's got a tail all right. One of you boys can warm me up, but I'm going to get me a black buck to do me right."

One of the white men, a man who wasn't laughing, jumped off his bar stool. "Get your dirty black hands off that white lady, you nigger bastard."

He kicked me right in the mouth.

One of the men who had been laughing came off his stool and grabbed the man who kicked me.

"For Christ's sake, he's just a little kid."

"Mind your goddamn business."

Whop. The fight was on.

The bartender jumped over the bar and grabbed me with one hand and my shoeshine box with the other. "Sorry, boy, it's not your fault, but I can't have you around."

Out on the sidewalk he gave me a five-dollar bill.

When I saw all the blood and pieces of tooth on
shirt, I got scared. Momma would be real angry. So
went over to Boo's house and spent the night. I told Bo
if I could get kicked in the mouth a couple more times
today, and get five dollars each time, man, I'd be all
right.

"What time is it, Momma?"
"Four o'clock, Richard."
"I guess I didn't have to burn them, did I?"

The tavern isn't so bad, Momma. No kid ever runs up
and laughs at me because I'm shining shoes. But they
sure remind me I'm on relief. And there's another reason
I won't quit working the taverns, Momma. In the winter-
time it's warmer in there, and in the summertime it's
cooler than our house. And even though men spit in my
face and kick me in the mouth, Momma, every so often
somebody rubs my head and calls me son.

"Why do you believe he's coming, Richard?"
"Oh, Momma, I talked to that Man in the back-
yard, I know he's coming."
"Go on to bed, Richard."
"No, Momma, I'll wait here with you. If I lay
over there in the chair, when he comes will you wake
me up?"
"Sure I will, Richard. Now get some sleep."
"Okay, Momma."

So many things I wanted to tell you that night, Momma.
There was a little girl used to wave to me when I cut
through the alley to get onto Taylor, a clean little girl
who used to sneak a piece of cake off her table and give
it to me. A piece of cake and a glass of Kool-Aid. After
a while, I'd finish up my paper route early just to come
back and wave at her. After dinner, her Momma and
Daddy would go up to the front room to sit around and
leave her in the back to do the dishes all alone. I started
to help her wash the dishes. I'd creep in up the back

...h and she'd let me in and say: "Sh, nobody knows ...u're here." It was like playing house. I'd just come and ...and there at the sink with her every night and help her with the dishes. Then one time her father came back to the kitchen. He grabbed me and he shook me and told me how I broke into his house because his daughter wouldn't let no dirty street kid in.

She was crying, scared to death, and she said: "I let him in, Daddy, I let him in, he's my friend."

"No, sir, she's lying," I said. "I make her bring me food out, I make her let me in."

He slapped me. He slapped me until I fell down, and when she grabbed onto his arm, crying and screaming to make him stop, he kicked me out the door to the back porch. He started to choke me.

Then he stopped. "Why you grinning at me like that, you little bastard?"

"Last week when you woke up drunk on this here porch, that was me brought you home. Found you on Sarah Street and brought you home and was so proud leading your black ass down the street 'cause you acted just like my Daddy would. Come out of your drunk every now and then, swinging and fighting. I had to run and duck. People see you and want to jump on you. But I tell them that's my Daddy, he's all right. Leave him alone, that's my Daddy."

He let me go, and he backed away and there was a funny look on his face. He started sweating, and chewing on his lip, and looking around to see if anybody heard what I had said. He opened his mouth, but nothing came out. Then he reached into his pocket and pulled out his wallet. He gave me a dollar. I threw it back at him. I reached into my own hip pocket and pulled out a dollar. My dollar was bigger than his because nobody knew I had mine. And then I walked away.

"God, my little Richard's asleep now and I have to talk to You. I always made a big mistake, God. I sit here every Christmas, times in the summer, too, and pray for his Daddy and never pray for other kids' Daddies. Send them theirs first, and then if You're not too weary, oh, Lawd, send Big Pres home. But when You send him, God, don't send him for me. Send him 'cause the boys need him."

"God, my Momma cried herself to sleep so I'm asking You to send Daddy home right away. God, wherever he is let him knock on that door. I'll wait up for him, God, just let him please knock on that door."

Momma, I loved those firemen in St. Louis, so big and tall and strong, rushing out to save people, Negro firemen and white firemen, no difference, they'd rush out and never ask whose house it was, how much money he had, if he was on relief. I'd stand on the corner where they had to pass and I'd wave to them, and sometimes they'd wave back. Sometimes I thought they went out of their way to pass that corner, just so they could wave to me. Then I'd follow them to the fire, and stand there and pray they would put it out fast so none of them would get hurt. I used to count every fireman that went up the ladder and count them as they came back down. Once I saw them use the net to save somebody and they didn't act like they were doing anybody a favor. I'd see them standing around in their uniforms, like they all belonged to the same family, and talk about fires. At the big fires, when the Red Cross came, they'd drink coffee and bite into sandwiches. It's a beautiful thing to watch a man who really deserves the food he eats.

One time I bought an old raincoat with hooks instead of buttons, and a pair of old hip boots. I hid them in the cellar. Nobody knew I had them. Whenever I wanted to feel good I'd put them on and walk around the cellar, pretending I was putting out fires, running up ladders to save people, catching people in my net. Then I'd take them off and walk over to the firehouse and watch them drill and clean the engine and roll up the hose. I'd walk right up to a fireman and say: "Excuse me, mister, but I shore like you all." He'd turn around and say some-

ng nice to me. Sometimes, before I knew better, I
ed to think my Daddy was a fireman somewhere, sav-
ng people and saying nice things to kids.

"Momma, Momma, wake up, wake up, Momma.
Didya hear it, didya hear it? Somebody's knockin'
on the door."

There was a neighbor woman standing at the door when
I opened it.

"Let me speak to your mother, Richard."

I left the room like I was supposed to when a grown
person came in. But I listened.

"He's here, Lucille, Big Pres been down my house all
night scared to come home 'cause he ain't got nothing
for the kids but some money. He just got in this evening.
Been over my place crying, Lucille, 'cause he went and
gambled and won and when he finished winning all the
stores was closed."

I ran right in and Momma grabbed me and hugged
me. "I told you, Momma, didn't I tell you he was coming? Go get him, Momma, go and tell him we got everything we want."

I ran back and woke up the kids—"Daddy's home,
Daddy's home"—and they tumbled out of bed, all five
of them rolling and fighting their way out of the blankets,
caught up in the sheet and scrambling around for the
socks they lost under the covers and bumping into each
other and in such a hurry they got legs and arms all
mixed up. But nobody was mad at all. We all ran into
the kitchen and jumped up and down while Momma got
dressed again, put on the fanciest of the clothes the
white folks gave her, clothes she never wore, and fixed
her hair and put on lipstick and perfume.

"You don't need that stuff, Momma, just go get Daddy
and bring him home."

After Momma left, we quieted down. We sat in the
front room by the window and we waited. We hadn't
seen him much in five years. We waited a long time because Momma hadn't seen him much in five years either.

"Aw, he's not really here," said Dolores. She w twelve. "Anyway, I don't want to see him."

"I want to see him," said Ronald. He was seven, and he was sitting on the floor, shivering, and holding onto Pauline's hand. Pauline was the baby, she was almost five.

"Oh, man," said Presley, who was fourteen, "I can't wait, he's gonna be so clean, a two-hundred-dollar suit on him."

"Dare anybody, he gonna be wearin' thousand-dollar suits," said Garland, who was nine. "And he'll have a pocketful of money."

"Yeah, a pocketful of money, but no gifts," I said.

"He been busy makin' money," said Garland.

"He's a soldier," said Ronald.

"Momma said he's a cook," said Dolores.

"Big deal."

"What's matter with you, Richard, don't you want to see Daddy?" said Presley.

"Last week I wanted to see him, when the rent man was cussin' Momma."

"He been busy makin' money," said Garland.

Pauline started to cry, and Ronald leaned over and rocked her in his arms. "Ooooh, you be quiet, little rat, you Daddy comin' home, he's a soldier."

"He's a cook," said Dolores, pushing Presley a little to look out the window.

"Shut up, girl," said Presley. "You remember when Daddy carry that old lady cross the street?"

"No."

"See, you don't know nothing. Man, was he ever big and clean. He got arms so strong he just picked this old lady right up after she fell off the streetcar and carry her cross the street and up to her house. Everybody saw it."

Presley did a lot of talking that night. I was just thinking. I thought about that time that trampy woman came by and shouted at my Momma. "Goddamn husband of yours home?"

"No, he's not," Momma said politely.

"I just want you to know anytime he ain't at your 〔h〕ouse or my house, he's at some woman's house."

"I appreciate you wouldn't come by here talking like this because the kids can hear you."

"I don't give a damn 'bout your kids. I got some kids for him, too."

Yeah, I thought, Big Pres is coming home. All those nights Momma kept the hallway light on after we went to bed. All those nights she listened to the police news on the radio, listening to hear his name. The times the police came by the house to ask if we'd seen him lately.

Suddenly a taxicab pulled up outside the window and we heard the door slam, and a big, deep voice like nobody's but my Daddy's was saying, "Keep the change, friend." And then all the kids were on their feet and knocking each other down to get to the door, and Ronald dropped Pauline, and everybody was hollering and screaming, and the last thing I heard was my Momma's voice saying, "Don't touch his clothes with your dirty hands, now don't touch his clothes."

I slammed the bedroom door and climbed into bed with my sneakers on and cried. I pulled the blanket over my head, but I could hear all right.

"Man, look at that thousand-dollar suit, see, what'd I tell you, Presley? . . ."

"Lookit, Daddy, lookit, Daddy . . ."

"Hey, Daddy, pick me up after Pauline. . . ."

"Now you get off Big Pres, don't go messing up his clothes with your dirty hands. . . ."

" 'Cille? Where's Richard?"

"Richard, Big Pres is here, come on out." But she was scared to leave him to see if I was okay. When she turned her back he might walk out again.

"Lookit all that money Daddy got. Bet it's a million dollars. . . ."

"Where'd you get all that money, Daddy? . . ."

I could hear him crackling the money in his hand and his big, deep voice saying, "You been a good girl, 'Lores, doin' like your Momma says. . . . You been good, Presley, don't want you growin' up to be like your Daddy now . . . payin' your Momma mind and doin' your school work. . . . How about you, Garland? . . ."

And I lay there and bit the cover and kicked the sheet and cried. Don't want you growing up to be like your Daddy now. Is that what he's worried about? I bit the cover until my gums started bleeding and I didn't stop until my nose was all stuffed up from crying. Don't you worry, Daddy, don't you worry.

After a while, Momma brought him into the bedroom. "Big Pres, Richard waited up all night for you, he knew you were coming. He bought you something for Christmas, Big Pres. You know, he buys you something every Christmas."

She pulled on me. She rolled me over. "What's wrong with you, Richard, didn't you hear me call for you, didn't you hear me say Daddy's home? What are you crying about, Richard, what's wrong with you?"

She didn't tell him what was wrong. No, you got to treat strangers with respect. "Big Pres, he's just jealous, he's just jealous 'cause you didn't pick him up like you picked up the others."

I lay in bed and I looked up at that man and he was ten feet tall. Tallest man I ever saw. He was clean, and he was strong, and he was healthy. He sat down on the bed next to me.

"Don't you sit on that dirty bed, Big Pres," said Momma, and she brushed off his suit and got one of the silk tablecloths the white folks had given her which we never used. She put the tablecloth on top of the sheet, yeah, the one sheet that stayed on the bed for six months. She didn't want Big Pres to get his suit dirty.

"I brought you some money, Richard."

"Don't want it, Daddy."

"Got more for you than I got for the others."

"Still don't want it."

"I'm your Daddy, boy, don't you want to see me?"

"I see you every time I see my Momma on her knees in front of the window cryin' and prayin' you'll come. You oughta thank me 'cause I brought you here, yeah, thank me you never get sick 'cause every night I say my prayers I say bless him wherever he is."

"Richard, I'm going to stay home with you this time, if you want me I'll stay home. You want me to stay, Richard?"

I didn't say anything.

"I'll get a job. Your Momma won't have to work. You want me, Richard?"

I looked at him but I didn't say anything. I guess he meant what he said. The moment he said it, anyway. And I lay there and I was thinking: If you stay, old man, I'll leave. I don't need you, Daddy, not now. I needed you when the boys chased me home, when the man cheated me out of my paper money, needed you every time Boo's Daddy came home at seven o'clock.

" 'Cille, what's wrong with this boy?"

"Don't you worry about him, Big Pres, he's crazy."

That got me mad, Momma forgetting all her love for me to pacify him.

"Yeah, he's crazy. Hey, 'Cille, you got a drink around the house?" She brought out the whiskey. He drank it right out of the bottle.

I got dressed that day and I left the house to play, but I ducked back every half hour to see if he was still there. Once I slipped Boo in to let him peep.

"That's my Daddy, Boo. My Daddy's rich, too, man, pocket full of money."

"Your Daddy ain't got no money. You all on relief."

"Come here, Boo, let me show you something." I walked up to my Daddy and looked at him. It was the first time I walked in and said anything to him. I didn't ask him, I told him.

"Give Boo five dollars, Daddy."

When he reached in and pulled out that pocketful of money, Boo's eyes popped out. He hadn't ever seen that much money in his life. Looked like he had all the money in the world. He looked so fine fumbling through those twenties and tens and fives, and I wondered if it was enough to go over to Mister Ben's and wipe out the back bill and put a little on the front bill.

"You got a good Daddy," said Boo.

I kept slipping back all that day, peeping in to make sure he was still there. Once I thought I almost caught him leaving, all dressed with his brown bag in his hand, but when he saw me he put it down. I'd slip in and I'd hear him telling Momma all the things he was going to do for her. Stay home. Get a job. Get off relief. Give up other women. Take Momma to all the night clubs. She wouldn't have to work for the white folks no more.

"Told you about working so hard for them white folks," he'd say. "Don't want my kids left in this house all by themselves."

She cried. "You mean it, Pres, you really mean it?"

"Yeah, 'Cille."

She got up off her orange-crate chair and put her hands on his face and kissed him.

I walked right in then. "Get your goddamn hands off my Momma."

He beat me, pulled off his belt and beat me across my backside. Momma held me on her lap while he beat me.

"Ha. That's a hell of a man there, that Richard. I beat his ass good, 'Cille, and he don't even cry."

He had little men and he didn't even know it. Every time he hit me I couldn't cry from almost wanting to laugh. I know, old man, couple of days from now you'll be too far away for that belt to reach me.

Momma made me go to bed and she whispered: "Please treat your Daddy nice. For me. Please do it for me."

"I'm the cause of his being here, Momma. I'm the one that asked the Man out back, I prayed for him."

"That's right, Richard."

That night he beat her.

He beat her all through the house, every room, swinging his belt and whopping her with his hand and cussing her and kicking her and knocking her down and telling her all about his women.

"Think you're so goddamn good, bitch," said my Daddy, cracking my Momma across her back with his belt. She whimpered and fell against a little table, knocking over a lamp from the white folks. She bent over to pick up the lamp and Big Pres kicked her in her backside and she fell forward on the linoleum floor. She lay there, her face pressed against the linoleum, sobbing.

"I don't even feel right walking down the street with you," he said, kicking her in the side with his foot. "Walk down the street everybody wants to run up, say hello to you, they look at me like I was dirt."

He grabbed her hair and pulled her up to her knees. Momma looked up at him, tears running down her cheeks. Slap. Right across her face. "I got bitches, women like you never seen, proud to walk down the street with Big Pres." Slap. Momma fell down on her face again.

"Get on your feet, bitch." Momma got up, slowly.

Whop. Momma spun across the front room, back toward the kitchen, like a drunk. Whop. Big Pres had the belt out again, and now he drove her in front of him, around the kitchen table, Momma stumbling over the chairs and the orange crates, Big Pres kicking them out of his way. Whop. Back into the front room, Momma bounced against a soft chair, then against the wall.

"And what the hell you taught Richard, bitch? Hell, whatever you taught him, you ain't gonna turn them all against their Daddy."

She never said a word, just crying, sobbing, trying to stay on her feet, trying not to get hit too hard but never really ducking his hand or his belt. She'd see it coming and close her eyes and put her hands up, but she never tried to get out of the way. The kids were crying and hollering and Ronald and Pauline were hugging each other and Dolores was hiding her face in her hands. Garland and Presley were scared to death. I watched him knock her down, and cuss her, and he was saying the things I wanted to say when she forgot her love for me and told him I was crazy. He left her on the floor, dirty and crying, came over and whopped me across my face so hard that when I knocked into the wall the pictures fell right off their hooks. One was a picture of Jesus, and the other was a piece of wood with the Ten Commandments.

And then they were in the kitchen and Big Pres was

crying and kissing my Momma and saying he was sorry and how he was going to take care of us and give up his women and get a job.

And Momma kept saying, "No, Big Pres, it's all my fault, it's all my fault, I shouldn't talk like that, they'll be time to get off relief when you're home awhile and get a chance to rest up."

I got up off the floor and I walked into that kitchen. Big Pres was sitting at the table with his face in his hands, and Momma was standing over him, stroking his head. They both were crying. I took down the butcher knife off the wall, the big one with the black handle, and swung at his head. Seen plenty of people swing knives in the taverns and I knew how to cut. Swung right at his head, everything I had, I swung for every kid in the whole world who hated his no-good Daddy.

Momma grabbed my wrist with both her hands and twisted the knife out of my hand.

Big Pres looked up real slow. I guess it's a hell of a thing for a man to look up into his own son's eyes and see murder.

"I'll leave now, 'Cille," he said very softly. "You should have let him hit me, should have let him kill me. I never was any good, never treated you or him right. I need to be dead."

He got up. "Don't beat Richard, 'Cille, don't beat him. I know what I done."

Momma grabbed Big Pres' leg and he kicked her away. He turned and walked out the door. My Momma tried to hold the door open while he closed it behind him.

"No, Big Pres, he didn't mean nothing, Richard's crazy, you know that. . . ."

He turned and kicked her foot out of the door, and slammed it shut. My Momma fell down and slid across the floor, holding the doorknob in her hand.

"Don't leave, Daddy, don't leave, Daddy . . ." the kids were screaming.

I followed him out the door and down the street. He didn't see me, his head was down, and he walked like

the greatest crime in the world had just been committed
against him. His head didn't come up again until he
walked into a tavern. I walked in behind him and stood
near the door where he couldn't see me. He walked right
up to a woman sitting at the bar. She was smoking a
cigarette and tapping her high heels against the rail.

"Where you been, Big Pres? I been waiting on you for
hours."

"I had to beat the bitch's ass for bad mouthing you,
Mollie," he said. "But I got a tough little man there,
Richard, you should see that little man, beat his ass and
he didn't cry."

"I been waiting all day, Big Pres. Don't you start telling me about some little bastard you got. Don't even
know if it's yours or the . . ."

"Watch your mouth, Mollie. My 'Cille's a good woman,
no loose piece of trim like you."

"Sure, who you think buys the bread when you're . . ."

He knocked that bitch right off the stool. He swung
that big hand of his and her cigarette went one way and
her shoes came off and she went face first on the floor.
He stomped that woman like no other man in the world.
I got to see my Daddy at his best that night. Two men
stood up from tables and started toward Big Pres. He
threw back his head and he laughed and he stood over
that bitch and his hand came out of his pocket with a
razor in it.

"Dare any dirty mother-fucker in this place to come
and stop me from stomping this bitch. Hear?"

Nobody moved.

He walked out of there, ten feet tall. My Daddy. I
walked over to the woman on the floor and helped her
up. She shook me away.

"I'm real sorry, ma'am."

She spat in my face. She didn't know I was Big Pres'
boy.

I watched him walk down the street, head up high,
hands swinging loose. Big Pres. A real Capone with the
whores and the bitches. Heard "I love you" from some
broad off the street. But never from his own kids. And

that's worth all the sevens falling on all the craps all over the world. He missed it. Missed seeing his kids grow up, missed having his kids crawl into bed with him and lie down and go to sleep because Daddy's sleeping. He missed what I have now. Feeling a little girl put a finger in my mouth, knowing that Daddy will never bite hard. Hearing a little kid say: "Throw me up in the air, Daddy," sure that Daddy will catch her.

Big Pres had to be a lonely man. There must have been times he woke up in a lonely bed, and wanted to give every whore he ever had, every seven, every eleven he ever threw, every wild time he ever had, just to go all the way back and have one of his kids walk up to him and say: "Daddy, I love you."

There must have been times like that. Because I would turn in all the Dick Gregorys in the world and all the night clubs and all the money just to go back to those days and find a Daddy there.

When you have a good mother and no father, God kind of sits in. It's not good enough, but it helps. But I got tired of hearing Momma say, God, fix it so I can pay the rent; God, fix it so the lights will be turned on; God, fix it so the pot is full. I kind of felt it really wasn't His job. And it's a hell of a thing when you're growing up and you're out on the street and you kind of hedge up to a man so he can rub your head and call you son. It's a hell of a thing to hear a man say: I wish my boys were more like the Gregory boys. If Big Pres could only know how people admired the Gregory boys.

Well, Big Pres walked away and left us. Left us to face the cold winters, the hot summers, the Easters with nothing new, the picnics with nothing in the basket. I wonder if it ever dawned on him that he fixed it so we couldn't even go to church one Sunday every year—Father's Day.

I should never have swung at him with that knife. I should have fallen on my knees and cried for him. No kid in the world, no woman in the world should ever raise a hand against a no-good Daddy. That's already been taken care of: A Man Who Destroys His Own Home Shall Inherit the Wind.

When I got back home that night, the knob was back on the door. And the light was on in the hallway. She was sitting up that night, looking out the window. Momma sat like that for the next three or four months, looking out the window, dozing in her chair, listening to the police news. Then she'd go to work without having been to bed.

Sometimes I'd stay up with her, listen to the radio with her, look out the window with her. I tried to make her believe I didn't know she was waiting on him.

II

Like a lot of Negro kids, we never would have made it without our Momma. When there was no fatback to go with the beans, no socks to go with the shoes, no hope to go with tomorrow, she'd smile and say: "We ain't poor, we're just broke." Poor is a state of mind you never grow out of, but being broke is just a temporary condition. She always had a big smile, even when her legs and feet swelled from high blood pressure and she collapsed across the table with sugar diabetes. You have to smile twenty-four hours a day, Momma would say. If you walk through life showing the aggravation you've gone through, people will feel sorry for you, and they'll never respect you. She taught us that man has two ways out in life—laughing or crying. There's more hope in laughing. A man can fall down the stairs and lie there in such pain and horror that his own wife will collapse and faint at the sight. But if he can just hold back his pain for a minute she might be able to collect herself and call the doctor. It might mean the difference between his living to laugh again or dying there on the spot.

So you laugh, so you smile. Once a month the big gray relief truck would pull up in front of our house and Momma would flash that big smile and stretch out her hands. "Who else you know in this neighborhood gets this kind of service?" And we could all feel proud when the neighbors, folks who weren't on relief, folks who had Daddies in their houses, would come by the back porch for some of those hundred pounds of potatoes, for some sugar and flour and salty fish. We'd stand out there on the back porch and hand out the food like we were in charge of helping poor people, and then we'd take the food they brought us in return.

25

And Momma came home one hot summer day and found we'd been evicted, thrown out into the streetcar zone with all our orange-crate chairs and secondhand lamps. She flashed that big smile and dried our tears and bought some penny Kool-Aid. We stood out there and sold drinks to thirsty people coming off the streetcar, and we thought nobody knew we were kicked out—figured they thought we *wanted* to be there. And Momma went off to talk the landlord into letting us back in on credit.

But I wonder about my Momma sometimes, and all the other Negro mothers who got up at 6 A.M. to go to the white man's house with sacks over their shoes because it was so wet and cold. I wonder how they made it. They worked very hard for the man, they made his breakfast and they scrubbed his floors and they diapered his babies. They didn't have too much time for us.

I wonder about my Momma, who walked out of a white woman's clean house at midnight and came back to her own where the lights had been out for three months, and the pipes were frozen and the wind came in through the cracks. She'd have to make deals with the rats: leave some food out for them so they wouldn't gnaw on the doors or bite the babies. The roaches, they were just like part of the family.

I wonder how she felt telling those white kids she took care of to brush their teeth after they ate, to wash their hands after they peed. She could never tell her own kids because there wasn't soap or water back home.

I wonder how my Momma felt when we came home from school with a list of vitamins and pills and cod liver oils the school nurse said we had to have. Momma would cry all night, and then go out and spend most of the rent money for pills. A week later, the white man would come for his eighteen dollars rent and Momma would plead with him to wait until tomorrow. She had lost her pocketbook. The relief check was coming. The white folks had some money for her. Tomorrow. I'd be hiding in the coal closet because there was only supposed to be two kids in the flat, and I could hear the rent man curse my Momma and call her a liar. And when he finally went away, Momma put the sacks on her shoes and went off to the rich white folks' house to dress the rich white kids so their mother could take them to a special baby doctor.

Momma had to take us to Homer G. Phillips, the free hospital, the city hospital for Negroes. We'd stand on line and wait for hours, smiling and Uncle Tomming every time a doctor or a nurse passed by. We'd feel good when one of them smiled back and didn't look at us as though we were dirty and had no right coming down there. All the doctors and nurses at Homer G. Phillips were Negro, too.

I remember one time when a doctor in white walked up and said: "What's wrong with him?" as if he didn't believe that anything was.

Momma looked at me and looked at him and shook her head. "I sure don't know, Doctor, but he cried all night long. Held his stomach."

"Bring him in and get his damned clothes off."

I was so mad the way he was talking to my Momma that I bit down too hard on the thermometer. It broke in my mouth. The doctor slapped me across my face.

"Both of you go stand in the back of the line and wait your turn."

My Momma had to say: "I'm sorry, Doctor," and go to the back of the line. She had five other kids at home and she never knew when she'd have to bring another down to the City Hospital.

And those rich white folks Momma was so proud of. She'd sit around with the other women and they'd talk about how good their white folks were. They'd lie about how rich they were, what nice parties they gave, what good clothes they wore. And how they were going to be remembered in their white folks' wills. The next morning the white lady would say. "We're going on vacation for two months, Lucille, we won't be needing you until we get back." Damn. Two-month vacation without pay.

I wonder how my Momma stayed so good and beautiful in her soul when she worked seven days a week on swollen legs and feet, how she kept teaching us to smile and laugh when the house was dark and cold and she never knew when one of her hungry kids was going to ask about Daddy.

I wonder how she kept from teaching us hate when the social worker came around. She was a nasty bitch with a pinched face who said: "We have reason to suspect you are working, Miss Gregory, and you can be sure I'm going to check on you. We don't stand for welfare cheaters."

Momma, a welfare cheater. A criminal who couldn't stand to see her kids go hungry, or grow up in slums and end up mugging people in dark corners. I guess the system didn't want her to get off relief, the way it kept sending social workers around to be sure Momma wasn't trying to make things better.

I remember how that social worker would poke around the house, wrinkling her nose at the coal dust on the chilly linoleum floor, shaking her head at the bugs crawling over the dirty dishes in the sink. My Momma would have to stand there and make like she was too lazy to keep her own house clean. She could never let on that she spent all day cleaning another woman's house for two dollars and carfare. She would have to follow that nasty bitch around those drafty three rooms, keeping her fingers crossed that the telephone hidden in the closet wouldn't ring. Welfare cases weren't supposed to have telephones.

But Momma figured that some day the Gregory kids were going to get off North Taylor Street and into a world where they would have to compete with kids who grew up with telephones in their houses. She didn't want us to be at a disadvantage. She couldn't explain that to the social worker. And she couldn't explain that while she was out spoon-feeding somebody else's kids, she was worrying about her own kids, that she could rest her mind by picking up the telephone and calling us—to find out if we had bread for our baloney or baloney for our bread, to see if any of us had gotten run over by the streetcar while we played in the gutter, to make sure the house hadn't burnt down from the papers and magazines we stuffed in the stove when the coal ran out.

But sometimes when she called there would be no answer. Home was a place to be only when all other places were closed.

I never learned hate at home, or shame. I had to go to school for that. I was about seven years old when I got my first big lesson. I was in love with a little girl named Helene Tucker, a light-complected little girl with pigtails and nice manners. She was always clean and she was smart in school. I think I went to school then mostly to look at her. I brushed my hair and even got me a little old handkerchief. It was a lady's handkerchief, but I didn't want Helene to see me wipe my nose on my hand. The pipes were frozen again, there was no water in the house, but I washed my socks and shirt every night. I'd get a pot, and go over to Mister Ben's grocery store, and stick my pot down into his soda machine. Scoop out some chopped ice. By evening the ice melted to water for washing. I got sick a lot that winter because the fire would go out at night before the clothes were dry. In the morning I'd put them on, wet or dry, because they were the only clothes I had.

Everybody's got a Helene Tucker, a symbol of everything you want. I loved her for her goodness, her cleanness, her popularity. She'd walk down my street and my brothers and sisters would yell, "Here comes Helene," and I'd rub my tennis sneakers on the back of my pants and wish my hair wasn't so nappy and the white folks' shirt fit me better. I'd run out on the street. If I knew my place and didn't come too close, she'd wink at me and say hello. That was a good feeling. Sometimes I'd follow her all the way home, and shovel the snow off her walk and try to make friends with her Momma and her aunts. I'd drop money on her stoop late at night on my way back from shining shoes in the taverns. And she had a Daddy, and he had a good job. He was a paper hanger.

I guess I would have gotten over Helene by summertime, but something happened in that classroom that made her face hang in front of me for the next twenty-two years. When I played the drums in high school it was for Helene and when I broke track records in college it was for Helene and when I started standing behind microphones and heard applause I wished Helene could hear it, too. It wasn't until I was twenty-nine years old and married and making money that I finally got her out of my system. Helene was sitting in that classroom when I learned to be ashamed of myself.

It was on a Thursday. I was sitting in the back of the room, in a seat with a chalk circle drawn around it. The idiot's seat, the troublemaker's seat.

The teacher thought I was stupid. Couldn't spell, couldn't read, couldn't do arithmetic. Just stupid. Teachers were never interested in finding out that you couldn't concentrate because you were so hungry, because you hadn't had any breakfast. All you could think about was noontime, would it ever come? Maybe you could sneak into the cloakroom and steal a bite of some kid's lunch out of a coat pocket. A bite of something. Paste. You can't really make a meal of paste, or put it on bread for a sandwich, but sometimes I'd scoop a few spoonfuls out of the paste jar in the back of the room. Pregnant people get strange tastes. I was pregnant with poverty. Pregnant with dirt and pregnant with smells that made people turn away, pregnant with cold and pregnant with shoes that were never bought for me, pregnant with five other people in my bed and no Daddy in the next room, and pregnant with hunger. Paste doesn't taste too bad when you're hungry.

The teacher thought I was a troublemaker. All she saw from the front of the room was a little black boy who squirmed in his idiot's seat and made noises and poked the kids around him. I guess she couldn't see a kid who made noises because he wanted someone to know he was there.

It was on a Thursday, the day before the Negro pay-day. The eagle always flew on Friday. The teacher was asking each student how much his father would give to the Community Chest. On Friday night, each kid would get the money from his father, and on Monday he would bring it to the school. I decided I was going to buy me a Daddy right then. I had money in my pocket from shining shoes and selling papers, and whatever Helene Tucker pledged for her Daddy I was going to top it. And I'd hand the money right in. I wasn't going to wait until Monday to buy me a Daddy.

I was shaking, scared to death. The teacher opened her book and started calling out names alphabetically.

"Helene Tucker?"

"My Daddy said he'd give two dollars and fifty cents."

"That's very nice, Helene. Very, very nice indeed."

That made me feel pretty good. It wouldn't take too much to top that. I had almost three dollars in dimes and quarters in my pocket. I stuck my hand in my pocket and held onto the money, waiting for her to call my name. But the teacher closed her book after she called everybody else in the class.

I stood up and raised my hand.

"What is it now?"

"You forgot me."

She turned toward the blackboard. "I don't have time to be playing with you, Richard."

"My Daddy said he'd . . ."

"Sit down, Richard, you're disturbing the class."

"My Daddy said he'd give . . . fifteen dollars."

She turned around and looked mad. "We are collecting this money for you and your kind, Richard Gregory. If your Daddy can give fifteen dollars you have no business being on relief."

"I got it right now, I got it right now, my Daddy gave it to me to turn in today, my Daddy said . . ."

"And furthermore," she said, looking right at me, her nostrils getting big and her lips getting thin and her eyes opening wide, "we know you don't have a Daddy."

Helene Tucker turned around, her eyes full of tears. She felt sorry for me. Then I couldn't see her too well because I was crying, too.

"Sit down, Richard."

And I always thought the teacher kind of liked me.

She always picked me to wash the blackboard on Friday, after school. That was a big thrill, it made me feel important. If I didn't wash it, come Monday the school might not function right.

"Where are you going, Richard?"

I walked out of school that day, and for a long time I didn't go back very often. There was shame there.

Now there was shame everywhere. It seemed like the whole world had been inside that classroom, everyone had heard what the teacher had said, everyone had turned around and felt sorry for me. There was shame in going to the Worthy Boys Annual Christmas Dinner for you and your kind, because everybody knew what a worthy boy was. Why couldn't they just call it the Boys Annual Dinner, why'd they have to give it a name? There was shame in wearing the brown and orange and white plaid mackinaw the welfare gave to 3,000 boys. Why'd it have to be the same for everybody so when you walked down the street the people could see you were on relief? It was a nice warm mackinaw and it had a hood, and my Momma beat me and called me a little rat when she found out I stuffed it in the bottom of a pail full of garbage way over on Cottage Street. There was shame in running over to Mister Ben's at the end of the day and asking for his rotten peaches, there was shame in asking Mrs. Simmons for a spoonful of sugar, there was shame in running out to meet the relief truck. I hated that truck, full of food for you and your kind. I ran into the house and hid when it came. And then I started to sneak through alleys, to take the long way home so the people going into White's Eat Shop wouldn't see me. Yeah, the whole world heard the teacher that day, we all know you don't have a Daddy.

It lasted for a while, this kind of numbness. I spent a lot of time feeling sorry for myself. And then one day I met this wino in a restaurant. I'd been out hustling all day, shining shoes, selling newspapers, and I had goo-gobs of money in my pocket. Bought me a bowl of chili for fifteen cents, and a cheeseburger for fifteen cents, and a Pepsi for five cents, and a piece of chocolate cake for

ten cents. That was a good meal. I was eating when this
old wino came in. I love winos because they never hurt
anyone but themselves.

The old wino sat down at the counter and ordered
twenty-six cents worth of food. He ate it like he really
enjoyed it. When the owner, Mister Williams, asked him
to pay the check, the old wino didn't lie or go through
his pocket like he suddenly found a hole.

He just said: "Don't have no money."

The owner yelled: "Why in hell you come in here and
eat my food if you don't have no money? That food cost
me money."

Mister Williams jumped over the counter and knocked
the wino off his stool and beat him over the head with
a pop bottle. Then he stepped back and watched the
wino bleed. Then he kicked him. And he kicked him
again.

I looked at the wino with blood all over his face and
I went over. "Leave him alone, Mister Williams. I'll pay
the twenty-six cents."

The wino got up, slowly, pulling himself up to the
stool, then up to the counter, holding on for a minute
until his legs stopped shaking so bad. He looked at me
with pure hate. "Keep your twenty-six cents. You don't
have to pay, not now. I just finished paying for it."

He started to walk out, and as he passed me, he
reached down and touched my shoulder. "Thanks, son-
ny, but it's too late now. Why didn't you pay it before?"

I was pretty sick about that. I waited too long to help
another man.

I remember a white lady who came to our door once
around Thanksgiving time. She wore a woolly, green bon-
net around her head, and she smiled a lot.

"Is your mother home, little boy?"

"No, she ain't."

"May I come in?"

"What do you want, ma'am?"

She didn't stop smiling once, but she sighed a little
when she bent down and lifted up a big yellow basket.

The kind I saw around church that were called Baskets for the Needy.

"This is for you."

"What's in there?"

"All sorts of good things," she said, smiling. "There's candy and potatoes and cake and cranberry sauce and"—she made a funny little face at me by wrinkling up her nose—"and a great big fat turkey for Thanksgiving dinner."

"Is it cooked?"

"A big fat juicy turkey, all plucked clean for you. . . ."

"Is it cooked?"

"No, it's not. . . ."

"We ain't got nothing in the house to cook it with, lady."

I slammed the door in her face. Wouldn't that be a bitch, to have a turkey like that in the house with no way to cook it? No gas, no electricity, no coal. Just a big fat juicy raw turkey.

I remember Mister Ben, the grocery-store man, a round little white man with funny little tufts of white hair on his head and sad-looking eyes. His face was kind of gray-colored, and the skin was loose and shook when he talked.

"Momma want a loaf of bread, Mister Ben, fresh bread."

"Right away, Richard," he'd say and get the bread he bought three days old from the bakeries downtown. It was the only kind he had for his credit-book customers. He dropped it on the counter. Clunk.

I'd hand him the credit book, that green tablet with the picture of the snuff can on it, to write down how much we owed him. He'd lick the tip of that stubby pencil he kept behind his ear. Six cents.

"How you like school, Richard?"

"I like school fine, Mister Ben."

"Good boy, you study, get smart."

I'd run home to Momma and tell her that the bread

wasn't fresh bread, it was stale bread. She'd flash the big smile.

"Oh, that Mister Ben, he knew I was fixin to make toast."

The peaches were rotten and the bread wasn't fresh and sometimes the butter was green, but when it came down to the nitty-gritty you could always go to Mister Ben. Before a Jewish holiday he'd take all the food that was going to spoil while the store was shut and bring it over to our house. Before Christmas he'd send over some meat even though he knew it was going on the tablet and he might never see his money. When the push came to the shove and every hungry belly in the house was beginning to eat on itself, Momma could go to Mister Ben and always get enough for some kind of dinner.

But I can remember three days in a row I went into Mister Ben's and asked him to give me a penny Mr. Goodbar from the window.

Three days in a row he said: "Out, out, or I'll tell your Momma you been begging."

One night I threw a brick through his window and took it.

The next day I went into Mister Ben's to get some bread for Momma and his skin was shaking and I heard him tell a lady, "I can't understand why should anybody break my window for a penny piece of candy, a lousy piece of candy, all they got to do is ask, that's all, and I give."

III

My best friend in those days was Boo. His real name is Charles Simmons and he's a teacher in St. Louis now. Boo. He was fifty years old when he was nine. He was born old. He used to sit on the curb and pull all the insides out of a loaf of bread, and roll it up into little white balls and line the balls up in a neat row on the sidewalk. Then he'd go down the line and eat the little white bread balls one by one. We'd sit and talk while Boo ate his bread balls, figuring out all the tough things we were going to do.

"Hey, Richard."

"Wha?"

"Let's go down the zoo and let all the tigers loose."

"Nah, that's no fun, Boo. Let's get that streetcar conductor, we'll set him on fire and we'll drop him into Mister Ben's icebox."

"Nah, let's go beat up Calvin."

Calvin was Boo's little brother.

Boo was really tough. All the gangs were always trying to get him to join, he was such a good fighter. And if he couldn't whip a guy himself, he had a lot of older brothers who could. Mess with Boo, that was like declaring a war. Boo never started fights himself, he was too lazy, but he kept me from being beat up a lot of times. I was the neighborhood sissy. Ran errands for everybody—even Calvin.

We had a lot of fun, Boo and I, rolling down the street inside of big truck tires, playing stickball with a broom handle and soda bottle cap. Goes even farther if you pack the inside of the cap with dirt, but you better not let the other team catch you doing that. Best game we had was snatch and run—you kind of walk slow down a street whistling and looking around with your hands in your pockets pretending you're just taking the air. Then you pass a fence that has a sign *Beware of Bad Dog*. You slither past it, snatch the gate open, and run. I think that's the reason I got to be so fast later on. You can break world records if you got a bad dog chasing you.

Once I was bitten by a Great Dane when we snatched a gate on Cote Brilliant Street. The owner saw us, so when I went down to the clinic, I couldn't tell them I knew which dog bit me. They would have taken me back there to pick up the dog for a rabies test and the owner would have told Momma what I had done. So I had to take the fourteen rabies shots.

Boo and I never pulled anything big for kicks. We cheered at fights and we egged guys on to things, but we were the first to run away when the cops came. There were Negro cops in the neighborhood, and they were tough. They were even tougher on us kids than the white cops because they knew us better and how we acted reflected on them. There was Big Black and Middlebrooks and Clarence Lee and Grimes, the toughest of them all. That Grimes could put seven cats from the corner in the hospital with two blows. Once he caught a kid drinking wine in the schoolyard and he smashed the bottle while the kid was drinking out of it. With a baseball bat.

Toughest thing Boo and I ever did was bomb the streetcar. We'd fill up paper shopping bags with the powdery dark dust that lays over St. Louis when it gets hot and dry in the summer. Then we'd stand at the corner with our shopping bags and when the streetcar came we'd swing the bags around and around like softball pitchers winding up and then, just when the streetcar stopped, we'd let our paper bags go. Blam. By the time the dust cleared, Boo and I would be under the porch, watching the people rub their eyes and try to clean off their clothes, listening to them cough and curse. And Boo and I would be laughing our heads off.

Most of the time, though, Boo and I just hustled. Saturday was our big day. We'd get up in the early morning before daylight and run out to the white neighborhoods, not the rich neighborhoods where my Momma worked, but the working people's neighborhoods. Depending on the time of year, we'd scrub steps, shovel snow, wash automobiles, and wash windows. A lot of times I went out with Presley, my older brother, or alone, because Boo's father was a chauffeur, and he didn't have to hustle so much. It was the windows I didn't like, standing out there on a second-story ledge, afraid to stay out there, afraid to come in and go out again on the next window. Sometimes I prayed out there. A couple of times I pissed in my pants.

After working the white neighborhood, we'd come back to the Negro neighborhood and haul groceries from about two o'clock to about four o'clock. After that we'd get out our shoeshine boxes and while we were walking around looking for customers we'd sell wood and coal. We'd steal it from anywhere, we'd pull down a fence for wood. That night we'd work the white taverns shining shoes, and then sell the Sunday papers until about three o'clock in the morning. Come home, get up at six o'clock to deliver more papers until about 9:30.

My biggest problem was figuring out what to charge people. I never wanted anyone to hate me over a dollar. I'd say: "Pay me what you think it's worth." Hardly ever did they pay me what I thought it was worth, and I'd walk away disgusted. But then I figured at least I could always go back there, those people didn't dislike me for overcharging them. But I got taken a lot that way.

After we finished selling papers, we'd clean up and go to church. I liked church, sitting there and listening to the sweet music, and the preacher shouting, and everyone dressed so fine and clean. The Negro church has always meant a lot to the Negro—it was his club, his social life, a place where he could forget about The Man downtown. For me, then, it was a place to get all wrapped up in a God who was stronger than any teacher, or social worker, or man who owned a second-story window.

We went to the movies a lot, too. Loved movies. Alan

Ladd and Humphrey Bogart. So cool. We used to walk
like they did and talk out of the sides of our mouths
like they did, and smoke like they did, sucking that last
puff right down to our toes. Went to the serials, *Spy
Smasher,* fifteen weeks to find out the good guy won.
Never missed a Tarzan movie. Used to sit there and
laugh at those dumb Hollywood Africans grunting and
jumping around and trying to fight the white men, spears
against high-powered rifles. Once we had a riot in the
movies when Tarzan jumped down from a tree and
grabbed about a hundred Africans. We didn't mind when
Tarzan beat up five or ten, but this was just too many,
a whole tribe, and we took that movie house apart, ran
up on the stage and kicked the screen and fought the
guys who still dug Tarzan.

We used to root for Frankenstein, sat there and
yelled, "Get him, Frankie baby." We used to root for
the Indians against the cavalry, because we didn't think
it was fair in the history books that when the cavalry
won it was a great victory, when the Indians won it was
a massacre. We always cheered for the American soldiers and booed the Japanese and the Germans. We
never noticed that there weren't any Negro soldiers on
the screen, even though we saw them on the street. My
favorite movie then was *Kings Row.* I was about ten. Figured out all by myself that the old doctor cut the rail-
road man's legs off because the young guy didn't love
his daughter and she went crazy. I was pretty proud of
myself for figuring that all out. I guess I should have.
Sat through it enough times.

We had joys back there in St. Louis, joys that made us
want to live just as surely as the pains taught us how
to live. There was Camp Rivercliff, in the Missouri hills,
where we sat around a campfire at night and sang songs
and visited caves where Jesse James had stashed some
bank money, and learned about brushing teeth and using
soap and water. I went there two summers, two weeks
each time. Reverend James Cook ran it. He'd pick us
off the streets and pack us in trucks and take us into the
clear air. The counselors were Negroes who had finished

high school and gone to college. I really liked them. If you messed up, they beat you but good.

But I guess the best thing we ever did was go to see the Muni Opera. Boo and I would walk and run half the day to get there, to sit up in the free seats for kids. *Carousel* and *Showboat* and *Roberta,* those were the kind of shows we'd see, the kind of music that really made you feel good. We'd sit up there and watch the conductors, so sophisticated in their tuxedos. We were so far away from the singers and dancers that we couldn't tell if they were white or colored. During the intermission we could walk down and watch the rich people smoke and talk and laugh. That was part of the show, too. Sometimes in the summer we'd go almost every night. It was almost like church. And then we could go home, and turn on the radio and hum along with the same kind of music we had heard at the Muni, and close our eyes and the kitchen would disappear and we could see the whole show, all over again.

I got picked on a lot around the neighborhood; skinniest kid on the block, the poorest, the one without a Daddy. I guess that's when I first began to learn about humor, the power of a joke.

"Hey, Gregory."

"Yeah."

"Get your ass over here, I want to look at that shirt you're wearing."

"Well, uh, Herman, I got to . . ."

"What you think of that shirt he's wearin', York?"

"That's no shirt, Herman, that's a tent for a picnic."

"That your Daddy's shirt, Gregory?"

"Well, uh . . ."

"He ain't got no Daddy, Herman, that's a three-man shirt."

"Three-man shirt?"

"Him 'n' Garland 'n' Presley supposed to wear that shirt together."

At first, if Boo wasn't around to help me, I'd just get mad and run home and cry when the kids started. And then, I don't know just when, I started to figure it out. They were going to laugh anyway, but if I made the jokes they'd laugh *with* me instead of *at* me. I'd get the kids off my back, on my side. So I'd come off that porch talking about myself.

"Hey, Gregory, get your ass over here. Want you to tell me and Herman how many kids sleep in your bed."

"Googobs of kids in my bed, man, when I get up to pee in the middle of the night gotta leave a bookmark so I don't lose my place."

Before they could get going, I'd knock it out first, fast, knock out those jokes so they wouldn't have time to set and climb all over me.

"Other night I crawled through one of them rat holes in the kitchen, would you believe it them rats were sleeping six to a bed just like us."

And they started to come over and listen to me, they'd see me coming and crowd around me on the corner.

"We don't worry about knocking the snow off our shoes before we go into my house. So cold in there, no snow's going to melt on the floor anyway."

Everything began to change then. Once you get a man to laugh with you, it's hard for him to laugh at you. The kids began to expect to hear funny things from me, and after a while I could say anything I wanted. I got a reputation as a funny man. And then I started to turn the jokes on them.

"Hey, Gregory, where's your Daddy these days?"

"Sure glad that mother-fucker's out the house, got a little peace and quiet. Not like your house, York."

"What you say?"

"Yeah, man, what a free show I had last night, better than the Muni, laying in bed with the window open, listening to your Daddy whop your Mommy. That was your Daddy, York, wasn't it?"

And then I'd turn, real quick, to another kid.

"Hey, Herman, did the police wagon ever get by your house last night? They stopped by my house and asked where you lived. . . ."

I got to be good, the champ of the block, the champ of the neighborhood as I got older. I'd stand on the corner, hands in my pockets, feet on the sewer lid, back to the street, Boo right next to me. After a while, they'd come from all around to try to score on the champ.

"You Richard Gregory?"

"Yeah."

"I'm George. . . ."

"You're midnight, blackest cat I ever saw, bet your Mammy fed you buttermilk just so you wouldn't pee ink."

Sometimes I could even use the humor on myself. Like when I was delivering papers and I broke my arm and I couldn't cry from laughing over the run-down heels on my shoes that made me slip when I turned the corner. A worn heel could break an arm, but I never heard of an arm could break a heel.

But mostly I'd use family jokes, about how my mother was such a bad cook, maybe the worst cook in the whole world. "Who ever heard of burning Kool-Aid?"

But that wasn't really very funny. There never was any mealtime in our house. If you were there, you ate. Grab a hot dog, a piece of baloney, bread, and run out again. Sometimes when the weather was hot, we were afraid to open the wooden icebox. The sour smell of yesterday's beans could knock you out. And it bugged me when the other kids in the neighborhood were called in to eat dinner. We'd be playing, and all of a sudden they'd all have to leave to eat. I'd just wait on their back porches until they were through eating and ready to come out to play again.

It's a funny feeling to be by yourself on a back porch and hear people eating, people talking. There's no talk in the world like the warm, happy talk of a family at the dinner table. I'd peep through the window and see my friend Robert in there, close by his Daddy. Then his Daddy'd get up and stick a toothpick in his mouth, pick up the paper, light a cigar, and walk around like he owned the world.

Once he came to the back porch, smiling to himself, looking at his cigar. Then he glanced down. And there I was.

"Who you, boy?"

"I'm Miz Gregory's boy, Richard."

"What you sitting out here for?"

"I'm waitin' on Robert to get through eatin'."

"Why didn't you come in and get something to eat?"

"I'm not hungry, thank you."

"You come on in here, boy, and get something to eat." He brought me in and sat me down at the table.

He brought me in the second day, too, and the third and that's when I thanked God for all the manners Momma taught me. Yes, sir. No, sir. Yes, ma'am. Thank you, ma'am. They looked pleased to have me there, too. The old man really dug me. Bet he wouldn't have minded it too much if I was his son, too. Damn, they all really dug me. Robert's little sister jumped up so quick to wash the dishes and bring me water that everybody teased her. "How come, Marjorie, you only show off and wash dishes when Richard's here?"

Then, on the fifth day, I met Robert's Daddy coming off the streetcar from work and I asked him what time you all going to eat. I didn't really ask him this because I was hungry. I asked him because I had sat at his table every day ashamed of how dirty I was, dirty from the top of my head to the bottom of my feet. This one day I wanted to go clean. Then I ran home and took a bath. I had polished my tennis sneakers and put them up on the roof so they wouldn't stink so bad. I washed my socks and ironed my shirt, and put on a pair of sissy short pants Momma brought home from the white folks. They were the best pair I had because I never wore them. Didn't like them, but I was really glad I had them. I wanted to sit at that table as clean as they were.

When I walked by the house nobody was outside so I knocked on the front door.

"Is Robert in, Miz Brown?"

"Yes, but he's eating now."

"He's eating now?"

"He'll be out after a while, you can wait on the back porch."

Then I heard the old man say, "Who was that out there?"

"That Gregory boy again."

"Little Richard, eh? Have him come in and get something to eat."

The table didn't seem as warm and happy that night. Robert's Momma was arguing with the Daddy about little things. After dinner, I helped them clear the dishes. I dropped one. Yeah, just my luck. I broke it. And when I saw the way Mrs. Brown looked at me, like I had no right to be there, I got a little mad. She didn't know I was going to bring her a whole set of dishes tomorrow, yeah, a whole set. Lunchtime I'm going by the ten-cent store and steal me a whole set of dishes and bring it to her in time for dinner tomorrow.

I was out on the back porch helping the old man sharpen his lawn mower when I heard it.

"Robert, I'm sick of that Gregory boy in here eating every night. Doesn't even say thanks any more. Ain't he got no mother and father?"

Goddamn. Now I'm crying. And now I start running.

And I run and I run and I run and then the alley ends and I turn out of that one and look for another. Didn't even say thanks. Yeah, I used to say thanks but you all made me feel so at home, like I belonged there with you. I never say thanks at home. You made me come off that back porch, you looked like you had so much fun and enjoyment with me there, you let me think I was part of the family, almost like one of Mister Brown's sons. Why'd she have to go say that? Ain't he got no mother and father?

IV

There were other fathers along the way, men who reached out and gave me their hands. There was Mister Coleman, principal of the Cote Brilliant Grammar School where I was transferred when I was thirteen. He called me into his office once when I was in the seventh grade. I walked right up to his big oak desk, and he leaned back in his swivel chair and looked me up and down.

"I've got a problem you might be able to help me with, Richard. It's about your job as a patrol boy."

"Sure, Mister Coleman."

"I've had complaints about how rough you are at the school crossing, Richard. You push the students, you use bad language. Now, I've watched you, Richard, and I know you're one of our best patrol captains. You don't let anybody cross until all the cars have stopped, you get right out there and make those trucks stay behind the white line. I don't want to have to take your badge away."

"Well, Mister Coleman . . ."

"How old are you, Richard?"

"Fourteen." I was embarrassed at being behind.

"You're a leader, Richard, a smart boy, a little older than some of the other students. They'll do just what you tell them if you're kind and strong. You've got to help them out on that corner, you can't be hateful. You're just like a father with a lot of children to watch after. Now go out there and keep those little kids safe."

At three o'clock I ran out on my post and stood out there like a happy traffic cop, as straight as a man could stand, proud because everybody was looking at me, because kids couldn't cross the street without me. Milkmen, laundrymen, they'd pull up their trucks and I'd

45

make sure all the kids were on the sidewalk before I'd wave them through. The drivers would lean out and wave at me and call hello as they passed by. I was somebody.

I changed a lot those years at Cote Brilliant. St. Louis had a segregated school system and that school had been built for white kids. But after the war, when the neighborhood changed, it became a Negro school. It had trees and lawns and a beautiful brick building. I had to walk through a nice neighborhood to get there from North Taylor. I stopped shining shoes that year because I wanted to go to school clean, without polish all over my hands. I started taking books home with me. I still didn't read them because it was too cold at home, but it was a good feeling to have them around. In the three years I went to Cote Brilliant, I only missed school when I didn't have enough warm clothes.

The teachers were different, too. I guess Mr. Coleman set the tone. They talked to me, they listened to me, I got a chance to see Negroes in authority who didn't seem bitter or out to get me. I got up in class and I talked, even if I really didn't have anything to say.

"Miss Carter?"

"Yes, Richard?"

"If two and two is four, then what you're really saying is that you have to subtract two from four two times to get zero. Or you could multiply two times two and then subtract it from four or from two plus two and still get zero. Isn't that right?"

"Uh, I think so, Richard, but perhaps you better say that again, slowly. . . ."

I never read books so I didn't really *know* things the way the other kids did, but all of a sudden I wanted to know. From all those years on the street I had a feeling that maybe there was more to things than just what was brought out in class. And so I tried to punch holes in the stories the other kids believed in ("I don't think anybody could throw a silver dollar all the way across no river") and show those kids they really weren't as smart as they thought ("Did you ever *see* that gold in Fort Knox, how you know it's really *there?*").

I didn't know the answers either, but I got to be a big man at Cote Brilliant. I got the reputation of a talker who could go on and on about anything at all. There was a school play about the United Nations, and I was invited to be an actor in it. I started to learn how to read the newspapers, and I could talk about the editorial page. And I was the big negotiator, the guy who broke up all the fights. Teachers would send for me to break up fights. Sometimes the big guys would come after me. A guy twice my size would grab me and push me against a wall and be all ready to knock my face in. I'd roll my eyes and look down at his feet.

"Baby, you better kill me quick. If you don't, I'm gonna steal those cool shoes you wearin'."

Now who could beat up a guy who said that?

Then I went to Sumner High and I was nobody again. There were a lot of wealthy Negro kids at Sumner, doctors' sons who had their own cars. Every girl looked as clean and smart as Helene Tucker. The athletes and the rich boys and the brains were the big wheels at Sumner High School. The only attention I got was in Pop Beckett's gym class. Pop was one of the first Negro graduates of Springfield College, in Massachusetts, probably the greatest physical education school in the country. He was tough. Rich or poor, everybody got hit one time or another in his class. He slapped me a couple of times for messing up, and it felt good to have somebody care enough to beat me for a reason. It got to the point where I started looking for it. Pop would stand up on the platform in front of the gym class, his face stony, his chest bulging out of his T-shirt, and I'd suck on my cheeks until my lips squeaked.

"Who was that?" Pop would roar.

"Me. It was me, Pop."

Whop.

Or I'd yell out: "Pop, you stink."

"That you, Gregory?"

"Yeah, Pop, it was me."

"Get up here."

Whop.

I became a big man in gym class because I was the only one who would yell at Pop and take my beating. I guess he knew why I was doing it because he never threw me out.

When school ended in June, Boo and Presley and I got jobs with the government flood control project on the levee. We told them we were eighteen years old. At $1.25 an hour, I figured I'd be able to get some nice new clothes for school next fall.

That summer was like a long bad movie. We had to load and pile sandbags up and down the banks of the Mississippi and it was so hot the soles of our boots got sticky and our shirts were like another layer of skin. Always wet, always muddy, and if you took your clothes off you died from sunstroke. We saw a lot of men die. Work all day, all night, puffing on cigarettes to keep the mosquitoes off, sleep where you drop, eat when the Red Cross truck came along with sandwiches and coffee. One of us always kept watch behind in case another man went crazy in the sun and started splitting heads with his shovel. We were loading hundred-pound sandbags one day and I'd been urinating blood for a week when the levee started shaking and the bags began to turn dark brown from the water seeping through. A Negro Army sergeant grabbed my arm.

"See my truck over there, boy? When the levee bust we ain't gonna pick up no whites, hear, but you hang near the truck and jump in."

And suddenly somebody was screaming: "It's breaking, it's breaking," and water and bags and men were spilling and tumbling around us and Boo and Presley and I were running through muddy water, running until we fell down and got up again. Once we were so tired we just fell down and stayed there. The water came seeping up through the ground and we were running again, no place to lie down, nothing to eat. We passed three white men standing on top of a rock eating cheese sandwiches. They wouldn't let us come up with them. One of them threw half a cheese sandwich down. Boo tore it in three parts and we were just about to bite on it when one of the white men grabbed his stomach and pitched over. We started running again. We got separated that night, and we didn't see each other again for a couple of weeks, when the water went down and we all were sent home.

We were heroes when we got home. Momma was so glad to see us because she had read about a truckload of Negroes who had been drowned. Boo and Presley and I strutted around the neighborhood, and people bought us watermelon slices just to sit on their front porches and tell them how bad it was, how many people we saved. We lied our heads off. It was beautiful.

We had a lot of trouble getting our checks for that summer. An old white man with a turkey neck down at the Federal Building kept telling Presley and me to come back tomorrow. Finally, Momma came down with us and straightened things out and a few weeks later we got almost $500. For the first time, Presley and I went downtown to shop in the big department stores.

We were treated like dogs. We'd go into a place and a salesman would hurry away from his white customer. "What do you boys want?"

"Hat."

"What color?"

"Brown."

"What's your head size?"

"Don't know."

"You have to know."

"I'll try it on."

"Like hell you will."

Wherever we went in the store, the detective would follow us. Couldn't touch, couldn't try things on. Funny though, they put our money right next to white folks' money in the cash register. We got home and we spread out our clothes on the floor for everybody to see. There were more shirts and socks and underwear on that floor than in the whole wide world.

I felt a lot better going back to high school that year, wearing new clothes, feeling clean on the outside. When I heard that the track team got to take showers every evening after practice, I asked the coach if I could join.

Sumner had the best Negro track team in the state and a brilliant coach, Lamar Smith.

"You run before?"

"Sure, coach, I do a lot of running."

"Where?"

"Around the neighborhood."

He shook his head. "We've given out all the lockers and uniforms for this year."

"All I want to do is take a shower in the afternoon."

He looked me over and kind of smiled. "All right. But you'll have to bring your own sweat suit. And stay off the track and out of my boys' way."

That's how I started in sports. Sumner had a fine athletic field. While the team ran inside the field, around the track, I ran outside, around a city block.

Every day when school let out at three o'clock, I'd get into an old pair of sneakers and a T-shirt and gym shorts and run around that block. In the beginning, I'd just run for an hour, then go and take a hot shower. And then one day two girls walked by and one of them said. "What's he think he's doing?" And the other one said: "Oh, he must be training for the big races." I just kept running that day, around and around the block, until every time I hit the pavement pain shot up my leg and a needle went into my side, and I kept going around and around until I was numb and I didn't feel anything any more. Suddenly, it was dark and the track team had all left. I could hardly walk home my feet hurt so much, but I couldn't wait until the next day to get out there again. Maybe I couldn't run as fast as the other guys, but I could run longer, longer than anybody in all of the city of St. Louis. And then everybody would know who I was.

I kept running all that fall and all that winter, sometimes through the snow, until everybody in school knew who I was, the guy who never took a rest from three o'clock until six o'clock. I don't think I ever would have finished high school without running. It was something that kept me going from day to day, a reason to get up in the morning, to sit through classes with the Helene Tuckers and the doctors' sons who knew all the answers and read books at home, to look forward to going a little faster and a little longer at three o'clock. And I felt so good when I ran, all by myself like a room of my own. I could think anything I wanted while I ran and talk to myself and sometimes I'd write stories on "My Favorite Daddy" and "What I'd Buy with a Million Dollars," and I could figure out why people did certain things and why certain things happened. Nobody would point to me and say I was poor or crazy; they'd just look at me with admiration and say: "He's training." I never got hungry while I was running even though we never ate breakfast at home and I didn't always have money for lunch. I never was cold or hot or ashamed of my clothes. I was proud of my body that kept going around and around and never had to take a rest.

After six o'clock I'd go to White's Eat Shop and wash dishes in return for dinner. Sometimes I'd go downtown and sneak into a white hotel and put on a busboy's uniform and get a good meal in the kitchen. The Man never knew the difference. "All niggers look alike." And then I'd go home and go to sleep because I was tired and I needed a rest. I'd be running again tomorrow.

When spring came, the coach called me over one day and asked me if I'd like to run on the track. I ran against the guys on the team, and they were still faster than me, but I could keep going long after they were pooped out. Every so often the coach would walk by and tell me I was holding my arms wrong, or that my body was at the wrong angle, or my knees weren't coming up high enough. But I was on the inside now and I was getting a little faster every day. By the time school closed in June I was beating the boys on the track team. The coach told me to report for track first thing in September. There would be a locker for me and a uniform.

That summer was the roughest I ever spent. The Korean War was on, and good jobs were opening up at ammunition plants. I lied four years, told them I was twenty-one, and went to work for a company manufacturing 105-millimeter howitzer shells. The unfinished shells weighed forty-five pounds each, and I had to pick up

:43 every twenty minutes. I always had stomach trouble, never could wear a belt, and every time I bent over and picked up a shell my insides tore a little. But with overtime I could pull down as much as $200 some weeks. When the other workers found out how old I was, there was a lot of resentment. They'd slip up behind me with crowbars and shove the casings down the belt faster than I could pick them up. I'd be so tired when I came home it was a real effort to get out and practice my running.

Then they put me on the night shift, eleven o'clock to seven in the morning. "Keep the streets a little safer at night, one less nigger running around," the foreman said. Now I did my running in the mornings after work, when the other folks were just going to their jobs. I kind of liked that, but it hurt not being able to be with Boo and my friends in the evening.

And then the foreman told another boss to put me down in the furnace pit. "Nigger can take heat better," he said. Well, the system wasn't going to beat me. I stood up next to that furnace, and I ate their goddamned salt tablets and just refused to pass out. They weren't going to make me quit, and I wasn't going to give them cause to fire me. I'd lean into that blazing pit until my face would sting, and when the lunch whistle blew I'd fall on the floor and vomit blood for half an hour and I'd clean it up myself.

It was all worth it. I could walk home at the end of the week and put money in Momma's hand. We could go shopping with cash instead of the green tablet; we could walk into a supermarket instead of Mister Ben's. I could stand at the check-out counter and listen to the cash register and my heart didn't jump with every ring. Momma could pay some back bills and buy some new second-hand furniture and some clothes, and not have to go to the white folks' every day. We had a little money around the house now, but we didn't sign off relief. It was too hard to get back on.

I kept my job when school started. The band had a special music class at eight o'clock in the morning, one hour before regular classes started, and I worked out a deal with the bandmaster, Mr. Wilson, to let me take it. That way I could come to school right from the plant, and finish up classes and track practice early enough to grab a few hours' sleep before leaving for the eleven o'clock shift. In return, I cleaned up the band room every morning, set the music out on the stands for the musicians, and kept out of their way. I liked sitting on the side and watching the band play, everybody working together to make a good sound, the bandmaster, a real sophisticated conductor with his baton, telling everybody when to come in, when to stop. I started watching the drummer. He seemed to be having the most fun, sitting there so cool, beating on that big kettledrum. When he brought those sticks down everybody heard him. He played all by himself, but he kept the whole thing going. I started tapping my hands on my knees along with him, and sometimes I'd get there a little earlier and take some licks on the drum myself. And after a while, when I was home, I'd keep time to the radio, beating a fork on one of Momma's pots.

After school I'd be out on the track, inside the fence with my own uniform. There was a new coach, Warren St. James. And he started spending a lot of time with me, teaching me how to start, how to pace myself, when to make that closing kick. I learned fast because I was hungry to learn, and when the season opened I was running in dual meets, in the mile and the half-mile. I was doing well, finishing third and second, and once in a while I'd win a little race. But I was always tired, sometimes too tired to sleep before I went to work at the plant.

Momma came into the bedroom one evening, about eight o'clock. I was sitting up in bed, thinking about last week's race and the mistakes I made, how I just didn't have it at the end, how I couldn't get those knees up high enough for the stretch sprint.

"Can't you sleep, Richard?"

"No, Momma."

"I don't know why you don't quit that old sport, Richard." She sat down on the bed. She always sighed

when she sat down. "I worry about you, Richard, you
got so much trouble with your stomach and your mind
drifts so."

"Momma?"

"Yes, honey."

"Remember when you took me to that old woman,
I was a real little kid, and she said I'd be a great man
some day."

Momma took my head in her lap and rocked back and
forth. "She saw a star right in the center of your head,
and I knew it, oh, how I knew it. You're gonna be a great
man, Richard."

"Momma, I'm gonna be a great runner, the coach said
I could be a great runner. Momma?"

"Yes, honey?"

"I want to quit my job."

And my Momma rocked me in her arms and I guess
she thought about the green tablet with the picture of
the snuff can on it, and getting up at six o'clock to put
sacks on her shoes and she said: "Okay, honey. And
don't you worry, my special little man, we're gonna be
all right."

That was my last night at work. The next morning
I got to the band room and the bandmaster was staring
out the window looking mad. There was a concert the
next week, and the drummer was in the hospital.

"You read music, Gregory?"

"No, sir."

"Well, I know you been fooling around with the drums.
Now I want to try something. Whenever I tip my head
toward you like this, see, I want you to hit the drum like
this, hear, and when I . . ."

The drummer never got his job back. We got through
that concert, and the one after that, and then it was
football season and I was banging the big bass drum in
the marching band.

Life really began to open up for me. Everybody in
school knew me now, the athletic crowd and the musical
crowd, and the girls that hung around both. I didn't go
out very much. I didn't have money, and I was pretty shy.

I could make quick talk outside the corner drugstore, or at a party, but when it came to that big step of asking a girl to have a date with me, I just couldn't get those words out.

But I was all right, man. The band was taking big trips, to West Virginia and Illinois and Kansas, and we were playing Beethoven and Bach and Mozart, cats I never heard of. Once, just once, I invited Momma to a concert. I sat on the stage of the school auditorium, and I got sick and ashamed when I saw her come in wearing that shabby old coat, her swollen ankles running over the edges of those dyed shoes, that dress the rich white folks gave her, a little too much lipstick, the cheap perfume. They asked her to go sit up in the balcony. I should have got up and thrown that kettledrum right into the faces of all those doctors and society people and light-complected snobs sitting in the orchestra. But I didn't. I just was glad she was up in the balcony where she couldn't be seen by too many people.

I never wanted her at track meets. That was mine, all mine. Flagpole Gregory, they called me, Ironman Gregory. I could run all day. I had style. I wore argyle socks in the races and a handkerchief wrapped around my head. I had a little trick. When I came down the stretch I'd look up at the flagpole and make a little salute. Then I'd go into my closing kick and win going away. They thought I was very patriotic, that the flag gave me extra strength. Once in a meet against Vashon High, the other big Negro high school in St. Louis, some kids took the flag down, figuring that would beat me. I never even knew it.

Most of the meets were on Saturday, and I'd stay out until ten or eleven o'clock Friday night, talking with Mister Ben, or walking with Boo, or hanging around with the guys at the candy store and the poolroom. They'd tell me about a fight they were going to have with another gang, or some little bitch they were all going to screw, and maybe some of the boys would come by with some wine. I'd tell them I couldn't make it, I was in training. I didn't tell them I didn't need it, I had something bigger going for me. Then, about eleven o'clock, when I was sure I was so tired I'd fall right to sleep, I'd go home.

I'd wake up early on Saturday mornings with a smirk on my face. I'd walk around the house, look at the peeling linoleum floor, the dirty dishes in the sink, all the raggedy shoes under the bed. I'd punch Garland on the arm and tickle Ronald and maybe pinch the girls. I'd hug Momma. "We're all right, Momma, we're all right." And then I'd take that one big step out of the house, jump the stoop, and I was in another world.

I'd walk to the stadium through the early morning, my uniform bag swinging in my hand, and with each step my stomach would turn over again and the little hairs would start standing up on the back of my neck. When I got to the stadium I'd just wave at the guard and he'd open the gate for me. I didn't even have to show him my competitor's pass. "Good luck, Greg, as if you need it." He'd wink at me and I'd wink back.

And the sun would be coming up high and it would still be cold under my sweater. I could feel the sweat under my armpits and between my shoulder blades and behind my knees. "Hey, Greg, hey, Greg," and I'd never look around, just climb quietly up to the grandstand and sit on a wooden bench like any other spectator. They'd be running off the shot-put and high jump early and I'd just sit up there and watch. Just another spectator at the track and field meet.

The loud-speaker would crackle and snap: "Will all entrants in the one-mile run please report to the official's table, will all . . ."

I'd stand up real slow, and feel this thing start to take me over, this monster that started at my toes like hot water flowing upward through a cold body. By the time I got down the steps I'd be on fire. I dressed fast in the locker room under the stands, put on my bright argyles, wrapped a handkerchief around my head. Then I'd walk out on the field and I knew I could crush the world.

"There you are, Gregory, I've been looking all over for you. Where you been?"

"I'm ready, coach."

St. James looked me over. "You better be. I want to talk to you. That big boy from Vashon, he's good, you have to watch his . . ."

"Don't tell me about him, coach. You go on over and tell him about me."

I got to the line with the other runners, and now, for just a moment, I was scared. God, I'm bringing 118 pounds of bones to this line, been training right, going to bed every night, trying to keep the rules, now . . .

Bang.

Let the pack get ahead of you for the first quarter, no need to get banged around and elbowed up there with the pace-setters burning themselves out. Take it easy, Greg baby, that's the way, that's the way. At the half they started falling back, the guys who don't know how to run, the guys who smoked, the guys who don't really have it. Take them now at the three-quarter, take one at the curve, get the other one coming off, and come around the straightaway and clean them all up. One by one. Don't play with them, Greg baby, don't play with them, just pass them by like snatching off weeds on the run like you used to do with Boo. Now you feel that thing, the monster, and you're going, man, you're going, ripping and running and here comes that bad dog. There's only two up front now and they're way over their heads, and here comes the flagpole, don't forget to look up and salute, Greg, that's your trademark. Somewhere Coach St. James is saying, "Goodamn. Look at that Gregory, look at that machine." And my knees are coming up higher and higher and I'm running faster and faster and I pass those two like the Greyhound Bus passes telephone poles and the tape snaps against my chest and then, slowly, I'm off the stride, slowly, my head goes down, and, slowly, the thing inside of me lets go. The monster slips out, and I'm left all alone there, Richard Gregory, not Dick, not Flagpole or Ironman, just Richard. I fall on my knees and then on my face, and the grass smells sweet and my stomach explodes. "That . . . that . . . my last race, coach . . . no . . . more."

"Come on, Gregory, on your feet. They're getting ready for the relays."

And I'm up again and waiting, and it starts all over, the hot water seeping up, the monster slipping back in. I can see our number three man hit the curve and slow down like I told him to and now I'm running and the stick hits my hand like an electric charge. I put my head down and I go and the charge stays with me because everyone else is ahead and they have to settle down and run a race, but I have to go out and catch them all. Now my knees are coming up again, higher and higher and higher than the flagpole, and I salute my knees and then I snap the tape again. This time, when I fall on the grass, I go right to sleep, into a dream world. I'm standing on the back of an open car riding up Fifth Avenue in New York City, ticker tape falling out of the buildings like a Christmas snow and everybody in the world is cheering me as I go by, except Big Pres who's hanging his head. I'm asleep in the middle of a stadium and I don't even hear them screaming my name.

I'd wake up screaming sometimes myself, my legs cramped and twisted under me. Momma would come in and sit down and take my legs and rub them gently.

"Anything makes a man like this here, he got to be crazy to go out and do it." she would say. "What is it, Richard, inside of you makes you go out there? I'm really afraid for you, Richard."

V

It was a thrill just to go to school, to walk down the street with guys and girls following me, jostling each other to walk next to me, to say: "Hey, Greg, how you feeling, baby? Gonna win the big one Saturday?" I'd just lay back and smile and wave my hand. Maybe say something funny about myself. That's all I had to do. Act nice, never put anyone down. They loved it, I was a celebrity. I'd walk into Mister Ben's and he'd stop whatever he was doing and ask me some question and make sure everyone in the place knew we were friends. If I said I was going out on Sunday to look over the track, there would be a crowd of little kids out there waiting for me. The same cop who used to come over and ask me what I was doing on the corner now came over and asked me *how* I was doing. The only one who never seemed too impressed was Momma. She had five other kids in the house and she wasn't going to let me get too big. I'd come running home, telling her the coach said I needed a special kind of food for my training. She'd tell me I'd better stop by the coach's house to get it.

"You don't understand, Momma. I'm putting the Gregory name on the map."

"Honey, I put you in the world, and the world was made before maps."

Only once did I ever invite Momma to one of my track meets. She refused. She knew I really didn't want her there with her shabby coat and swollen legs, sitting with the doctors' sons and the Helene Tuckers who cheered and screamed for Flagpole Gregory, the gladiator. I could almost hear them think—-After you kill that lion and stomp that elephant I'll bring you home, you running and you can tell us what the victory was all about .le we sip tea. But don't come too close

I took one of those girls to my first prom.

That was a big event in my neighborhood, getting me ready for that junior prom. I couldn't rent a tux because you had to leave a suit as deposit, and I didn't have a suit. But, somehow, Momma came up with the tuxedo pants and the white jacket. The white folks she worked for sent over a flower for the girl. I didn't know you were supposed to bring a flower. Momma took half the day off just to dress me, hollering, "Hold still," while she put the collar stays in. I was like a king with his court, my brothers and sisters standing around, watching me get dressed, crawling after studs that fell on the floor, opening the door for neighbors who wanted to see me. Man, I looked good in that tux. Didn't have to worry about the pants too long, the shoes not right, the tie doesn't match. Formal. It's there. You know you're perfect.

For an hour, Momma sent me around to Missis Rector's and Missis Simmons' and Aunt Elaine's, all over the neighborhood so folks could get a look at me. Mister Ben closed his door and pulled the shade and told me all about his first prom. Never knew he went to a prom. He gave me two dollars. Then Momma gave me five dollars and told me to stop by the Chinese place on my way home and bring back dinner for the family. We were going to splurge and have a party after I got back.

I didn't have fun at that dance. I was so afraid the taxi wouldn't stop for me that he almost didn't. The girl's mother and father looked at each other and started whispering when I went to pick her up. When we got to the prom she kept going to the bathroom with other girls, talking in a low voice with the doctor's son. She didn't want to dance to the blues, the gut bucket, the funky songs. Her crowd just came out on the floor for the sweet ballads. They talked about vacations and cars and clothes. After a while I went down to the far end of the gym and talked to the guys on the track team. Told them all about the women I screwed, the whiskey I could drink, the cats I had cut. Told them about this affair I had last week where the bitch screamed she would kill herself if I ever stopped giving it to her. Her husband almost caught us, but I climbed out a back window with her drawers in my hip pocket. I told the guys all the stories I had overheard in the taverns.

When the dance was finally over, a chilly fright came over the whole place. Suddenly, everyone who wouldn't talk to me or dance with me wanted to leave with me. When we walked out the door I found out why.

There were hundreds of them out there, all the cats who couldn't make it, the guys who couldn't get dates, whose processed hair was too long, whose pants rode down too far on their hips. The line ran for blocks, mean-looking guys just waiting. We went down the steps, and one of them knocked the doctor's son's hat off. When he reached down to pick it up, he got kicked right in his face. Then the fight started. I took my little group back inside.

From the window, I could see a mess of pink and blue formal gowns, rust-colored pegged suits, black and white tuxes, and greasy jackets boiling around together like a pot of beans and fatback. Society was paying its dues. Girls were rolling around on the ground with their gowns up over their heads, and a guy was running down the street with his tails split up to his neck. That was pretty funny. The hoodlums were having their ball now, downtown hoodlums pounding guys as they came out the door, and neighborhood hoodlums getting second licks, and the cats who just didn't have it standing around and cheering and ripping the dress off a girl now and then. One girl stood there just in her underwear, her yellow gown down around her feet, while her date, who had lost a shoe, was hopping away down the street. The cops were there, but they were pretty busy keeping from losing their hats. The only guys really fighting the hoods were the cab drivers, who were angry at losing all their customers.

While I watched, the boys on the football team, who had played against those hoods, been down in the nitty-gritty dirt with them, stepped out with their dates. They marched right through the line and nobody bothered them. So I took my little crowd out. The biggest downtown hoodlum looked up from beating some guy's head.

"Richard Gregory, hey, there's Flagpole Gregory. Come on, baby, you're all right." That big cat looked me in the eye, then looked at the crowd behind me. "You and your lady can go through, baby, but that's all."

The other cats stopped for a minute and looked up at me while the chief was talking, while he was really saying: Man, you're the same as we are and we're proud of you, but don't try to get anybody through because you should be out here fighting them with us.

The rest of my crowd broke and ran, and my date and I walked like a king and queen past the gang boys and the petty cats, through the bricks and the noises and past the hood who stuck his head out of the back seat of a police car and waved his handcuffs and yelled: "I'll get you next year, you . . ." to all the tuxedos he hadn't ruined this year.

We took a cab with some other people from the dance to the DeLuxe, one of the best Negro restaurants in St. Louis. I had heard about the place. A plate of shrimps cost two dollars and something there. I had Momma's five dollars left in my pocket after the cab rides. The crowd my girl knew were all sitting at one table, and they pulled out chairs for us kind of slow.

The doctor's son, who had been kicked in the face, looked me over. "You look pretty clean, man."

"Got punched a couple times, but I was lucky," I said. But he knew.

Then it started, from the far end of the table.

"There's a bug at this table, don't you see the bug?" I looked for the bug.

"Is it a big bug?" said somebody at the other end.

"You know it," said the far end.

"How you know it's a bug?"

"Smells like a bug."

After a while, when I realized they were talking about me, I picked up the menu and held it in front of me. It was like opening a box and seeing the most horrible face

in the world staring back at you. The cheapest thing
the menu was chicken. $1.25.

"I'll have the shrimps," she said.

I didn't even know what they looked like. I got scared
and I thought about the five dollars in my pocket. Some
of it was supposed to buy dinner for the kids. No choice.
I had to spend. I ordered the chicken.

I ate the chicken and the pie à la mode and I drank
the Pepsi-Cola, but I never tasted them.

"They wouldn't let a bug in this place."

"If it had a tie on, they would."

"Bug crawled right through the fight."

"Didn't get squashed?"

"No. Bugs never step on bugs."

I needed the final say that night. When the waitress
came over with the bill for the table, I looked up at her
and said: "I'll take it." The table got very quiet.

"I want to tell you, you did a real nice job here on
service. I've worked in white hotels and this is the best
restaurant I've ever been in."

The waitress puckered up her lips and put her hands
on her hips. "Son of a bitch, will you just give me twelve
dollars and fifty cents so I can get the hell out of here?"

I played my game. "Dammit, bitch, you cursed me.
You cursed me in front of my friends here, in front of
these ladies." And then I started to curse, my whole childhood spilling out of my mouth, everything vile I ever
heard on the street or in a tavern or from Big Pres. The
waitress' mouth dropped open and the kids started to
get up from the table. My date started to cry. She wanted
to go home. I gave her a dollar to go home in a cab.

The waitress was shaking. "Just give me my money,
you dirty little mother-fucker."

I whispered to her: "I ain't got no money."

She shouted: "You ain't got no money?"

Everybody heard her as they walked out of the restaurant.

"I'm sorry. I said all those things to stall for time.
Here's four dollars, your money for the service. I'll come

tomorrow. If I don't have money then, I'll wash ~~~es for it. Tomorrow."

She looked at me, and somewhere down the line I ~~~uess she could see what it was all about. "Okay. I be- lieve you."

When I walked out on the street, my date was still there. Crying. I took her home. When we got to her front door she turned around and leaned up against me. "Thanks," she said, "I had a lovely time." She wanted to kiss me good night. I couldn't believe it. She was the first girl I ever kissed.

I got back home that night about 4 A.M. The folks were sitting on my front porch waiting on me. And I lay back and smiled at them and waved my hand and sat down and told them all about the dance. The way it should have been.

I made them cry. The tears rolled down their faces when I told them how the girls in pink and yellow floated like clouds to music sweet as a chorus of angels. The guys were so strong in their black and white tuxes. I told them about the snowy white tablecloths at the DeLuxe, and how the shrimps were as big as my fist. None of us knew that the batter wasn't part of the shrimp. The waitress smiled and bowed, the cab drivers lined up to pick us up, we laughed and sang and strutted down the avenue like kings and queens, like high society. Me and the doctor's son got along so well he invited me over to his house next week. I showed them the lipstick on my handkerchief and told them how my date loved me, how elegant and fine she thought I was. They sat on the front porch and cried for what they had missed and I cried be- cause I knew they hadn't missed anything at all.

Then I went inside to face Momma.

"Garland cried all night," she said. "He didn't have anything to eat."

I sat down next to her at the kitchen table and told her I spent all the money. She cried.

"Did you have fun, Richard?"

"I had fun here before I left, Momma, all the folks coming by to see me. Had fun out on the porch telling

Boo and everybody about the dance I'm going to one day."

She put her arm around me. "It's my fault, Richard. I know kids don't go to that kind of dance without having twenty dollars in their pockets. I should have borrowed more."

"No, Momma, twenty dollars wouldn't have been enough for me tonight. I still would've messed up. I would've had to pick up all the checks in that whole restaurant, Momma, I would've had to pay for everybody."

There were other proms after that, and I learned what to do to have fun, to take girls who wanted to be with me, who wanted to dance to funky songs. I learned to slip out of the dance two hours early and buy some wine for the meanest cat standing outside. He'd get drunk then and dog somebody else a little more, but he'd let my crowd through. And I learned to introduce my girl to the hoodlum chief. That's all he wanted. When we left the dance he'd make all those cats stop fighting for a few minutes. Now that he and my girl were acquainted, he didn't want her to see him acting so badly. And by my third prom I figured out how to stop the beatings altogether. I opened the windows so the cats outside could peep right in. I brought special guys and girls by the windows and introduced them to the hoods. After a while those cats would whisper to one of my friends, "Hey, dance with that girl over there for me," and before you knew it, they were passing their bottles through the window and saying, "Have a drink on me, man." The guys on the outside were in on the party, too. And they acted nice because they didn't want those windows pulled to shut them out.

VI

That was a long summer, the summer of 1951. I was waiting for the scholastic record book to come out. In the spring I had won the mile in 4 minutes 28 seconds at the Missouri state meet for Negroes, one of the best high school times of the year, and I could hardly wait to see my name in the book when it came out in the fall. It was a long summer, and a hot one. The papers always had pictures of people frying eggs on the sidewalk in front of their houses. The mud on the river banks baked into a powdery dust that blew all over the city. All through June and July, Boo and Presley and I went downtown looking for jobs. Every day. Never got anything. "Sorry, boys, we're not hiring colored today." By August, Boo and Presley gave up. But I couldn't go back to shining shoes and running to the store for the neighbors. My name would be in a book soon. I kept going downtown alone.

It hit 109 degrees one day that August, so hot that skin peeled off my hand when I held a brass door handle too long. I had a nickel in my pocket that day, no job, and I started to walk home. Forty-five blocks, and every time I took a breath, the heat got caught in my throat. I thought I was going to pass out. And then I saw a beautiful sign on a restaurant window—AIR-CONDITIONED—SODA WATER 5c. It was cool inside, and the soda jerk looked like an angel in his clean, white uniform.

"We don't serve niggers here."

I just stood there, trying to get my mouth wet enough to tell him what I'd gone through that day . . .

"What'sa matter, you deaf, boy?" . . . to tell him how good it felt in here, to tell him I was sorry I was a Negro.

66

Someone in the corner smashed a pop bottle the marble counter and came toward me.

He came around in front of me, waving the br_ bottle in his hand like Humphrey Bogart would do the movies. There were others in back of him, grinnin_ He shoved the broken bottle at me, and I put my hand in front of my face. I didn't feel anything, but they started yelling. The soda jerk came flying over the counter like Alan Ladd, and he and Humphrey Bogart threw me out.

I started walking again, choking on the heat and the dust, watching my blood run down the sidewalk and the insides come out of my hand. It was white. Then I fainted. A wonderful feeling, like falling away from the world.

When I woke up, a white lady was kneeling in the gutter next to me, her arm under my head. Her other hand was stroking the lump on my forehead where it hit the pavement. "Everything will be all right, you're going to be all right, young man."

There was a white policeman standing next to her, and I tried to tell them that I wasn't bothering the lady, that I hadn't touched her. But my mouth was still too dry.

"Leave him alone, lady, I'll take care of this. The ambulance'll be right here."

"Where are you taking him, officer?"

"The nigger hospital."

"I beg your pardon?"

"Homer G. Phillips."

"That's too far. We'll take him to Barnes."

"Barnes ain't for niggers, lady. You'd better mind your business."

"Officer, do you know who I am?"

"Some nigger-lover who . . ."

The lady said her name then and the cop's mouth dropped open and he took a step backward. "I have your badge number and you can consider yourself fired." The cop began to apologize and help me into the ambulance. The lady got into the back with me. "Barnes Hospital, and quickly, please, this young man is seriously injured."

turned on the siren. For me. Cars got out of the
When she took me into the lobby of Barnes Hos-
I was a little ashamed of all the blood and dirt on
clothes. I had heard of Barnes, but never expected to
inside. They treated me well. Right upstairs, no wait-
ng, one doctor to clean my hand, another to sew eight
stitches and put on a clean white bandage. They all
seemed to know the lady, and she stayed with me all
the time.

Afterwards, she took me downstairs and called a cab.
The driver looked at us strangely, but the lady got right
in. She asked me where I lived, and she told the driver.
She kept talking to me the whole ride, but I didn't hear
a word. I just kept staring at the beautiful white bandage
on my hand. Nobody in my neighborhood had ever had
such a beautiful white bandage.

"I think I better get off here, ma'am."

"But this isn't North Taylor."

"I know, ma'am, but my Momma would think I did
something wrong if she saw me come home with a white
lady." That was true, but I couldn't tell her I wanted to
slip in the back door and surprise everyone with my
bandage.

"Are you sure you'll be all right?"

"Yes, ma'am."

"Are you really sure?"

"Yes, ma'am, and thank you very much. Thank you,
too, sir," I told the cab driver. When I got out, the lady
waved to me through the back window.

I started to run. I felt so good I ran five blocks, then
ten blocks past my house. Finally, hot, my hand throb-
bing, I went home. I slipped in the back door. "Hey,
everybody, come in here, you want to see something, you
really want to see something?"

Momma put me to bed and I stayed there for three
days. I only got up to put white shoe polish on my
bandage when it started to get dirty. Everyone came to
see me, and I told them about the white lady and the
ambulance and going into Barnes Hospital. I didn't know

the lady's name, and I think some people didn't believe
my story.

After a week or so, Momma told me to go to the City
Hospital to have the stitches removed. I didn't want to
go there, but nobody at Barnes had said anything about
my coming back. So I took the stitches out myself. One
by one, with a needle and scissors. It wasn't that hard.

That September the scholastic record book came out and
my name wasn't in it. I went down to the Board of Education and a man told me that records set in all-Negro
track meets were never listed. Coach St. James told me
the same thing. You have to run with the white boys to
get your name in the book.

The next time I went down to the Board of Education
I took a couple of thousand friends with me and I got
my name on television and in the *St. Louis Post Dispatch.*

What really happened was that the Sumner High PTA
organized a march on the Board that September to protest overcrowded conditions. There were a lot of ten-
sions and fears. Pop Beckett stood in front of the school
with a baseball bat in his hand and when he saw me he
told me not to get involved.

"Got to go, Pop. My Momma doesn't know I was one
of the best milers in the country this year."

He just looked at me, amazed.

My job on the march was to run up and down the
line, keeping the kids in order and warning them not to
steal from fruit stands along the way. The line got longer
and longer, as kids from other Negro high schools joined.
I never did get a chance to talk to the Mayor about my
time for the mile. The newspaper and television reporters
along the way thought I was kidding when I said I was
protesting because my name wasn't in the scholastic
record book. So I told them how there were eighty kids
in the English class, and we learned math in the machine
shop because there weren't enough rooms in school, and
the last ten kids to get to History had to stand up for an
hour because there weren't enough seats. They wrote in

ne papers that I was the leader of the demonstration. It's not as if I really *told* them that.

The police broke up the demonstration at Locust Street, in front of the Board building. They said it was a breach of the peace. And a man came out and told us that if we wanted better schools we should return to them. And another white man said that six adults from the PTA could come into the building and discuss the matter if the rest of us went back to classes. We did. The city was pretty well turned upside down by all this Negro marching and chanting and sign-waving. It wasn't even a matter of wanting to sit down. Back at school everyone told me I was going to get expelled, and back home Momma was all upset. The white folks had told her that the march was Communist-inspired. I told her I didn't even know how to spell Communist.

Nothing much happened right away, but the next week the high school cross-country program was integrated. I don't know if it had anything to do with the march. It was the first time Negro and white ever competed against each other in the high schools of St. Louis, and things really began to open up for me.

It was wild. There were rumors and excitement and electricity in the air. We didn't know the white boys and they didn't know us. We'd never had a chance to love or hate each other on a man-to-man basis, to watch each other run, to see each other naked. There were Negro rumors that the white boys had special conditioning and food that gave them the strength to beat us in the long distances. There were white rumors that we needed only three runners at a track meet: one would win the 100 and the 220, the second would win both hurdles, and the third would win the half and the mile. Then the three regulars would borrow a Negro water boy and win the relays.

My first integrated meet was a cross-country run over at Wood River. I was so nervous I was shaking when we came to the line. Coach St. James had given us a big buildup for weeks. He had made us learn strategy all over again, made us promise to lay off the grandstanding. No

argyle socks, no saluting, no crossing the tape ho
your buddy's hand, no waving at your girl friends.
was big time. If we won we'd get our names in the wh
newspapers the next day—we wouldn't have to wait unt
the *Argus,* the weekly Negro newspaper, came out on
Thursday. And the coach had told me that there was a
little white boy in the race who had one of the best
scholastic three-mile times in the country, and if I could
beat him I could win the race. But we had never run
the course before. And we didn't even know which was
the white boy to beat.

Bang.

I didn't break out too fast. Let the pack go on ahead,
this is a long race. You could see right away how different it was, running against boys who had eaten better
and taken better care of their bodies all their lives. They
looked smooth, they ran smooth. I moved up into the
pack, and then went on ahead. I didn't know any of
these white boys, which were the early pace-setters, which
were the ones saving themselves for a final sprint. So I
decided to stay with the leaders. There was a little white
boy way ahead of everyone else, running as easy as flowing water. He took the corners sharply, and never seemed
to get scratched by the bushes along the course. I got
scratched all the time. I decided he had to be the white
boy to beat.

I moved up, past the leaders, and started to dog that
white boy. He was running too fast for me, and when I
tried to match his pace my breath got short and it felt
like somebody was sewing up the left side of my stomach
and there was broken glass inside my shoes. He kept running easy. I knew I could never outrun him. Have to
trick this race, Greg.

About the two-mile mark, I came up alongside him and
slapped him on the butt. "Nice going, baby," I said, and
I fell back fast so he wouldn't hear me panting.

A little bit later I came up again and kicked him on
the heel of his shoe. Not enough to break his stride or
bother him or get myself disqualified. Just enough so I
could say, "Excuse me, baby." Again I dropped back fast

wouldn't hear my breath come out. That upset him,
he didn't break.

Not much time left now. Last chance. I came right up
behind him and I held my breath. He felt me running
right behind him and he heard my feet, but he never
heard me breathe. There was a fire in my chest, and my
mind got fuzzy, and when I tried to take a shallow breath
my brain kept clicking to shut it off, but he was looking
around him now and his eyes were wide and he was so
scared he speeded up. I held my breath as long as I
could, then I dropped back to where he couldn't hear
me and I let it all out and got myself together again. He
had speeded up too early, and when he tried to slow
down and settle back into his pace his smooth stride was
broken, and he was off. He was destroyed. He wasn't
running his race any more; he was scared and his mind
was all messed up.

I came up again and I knew I could pass him any time
I wanted to, now. But I didn't know the course, and I
didn't want to take the chance of making a wrong turn
and getting disqualified. So I stayed a few yards behind
him until the last 200 yards, a straight shot to the tape.
I could see the officials and the band and the crowd and
the photographers and I passed him going away, and
watched my knees all the way down the stretch, higher
and higher, right through the tape. And then I got to see
how Whitey treats his heroes.

First-class all the way. Had my picture on the front
page of the Wood River paper, and on the sports pages
of all the white St. Louis papers. Dick Gregory. No. 1.
That was the start of a hell of a year, that last year in
high school. I won the state cross-country meet at Forest
Park, white and Negro. State champion. And then I
finished second in a fifteen-mile race, the only high school
runner in a field of college boys. People started listening
to me that year, taking me to dinners, giving me awards.
Outstanding citizen. They always introduced me as Dick
Gregory, a boy who was born and raised on relief. Look
at him now, they said. As if relief was all in the past, as
if Momma wasn't still dragging home from the white

folks, as if I wasn't taking five dollars at a time out of her pocketbook. I was too busy being a good example to go out and work, to be much of a son or a brother.

I took the high school cooking course that year because I wanted to learn etiquette. I was getting to be a big man around and I wanted to learn how to hold a knife and fork. I always used to eat one course at a time, clean off the meat, then turn the plate and clean off the potatoes, turn it again and clean off the greens. I had to convince them at Sumner that I was going to be a cook after graduation so they would let me take the home economics course. That meant I had to take sewing, too. But I learned how to eat right. I never told them the real reason I took the course, so they put COOK after my name in the yearbook.

Didn't matter. I was captain of the track team that year, and the cross-country team, and I played the kettledrum in the orchestra and the bass drum in the band, and the bongos for a dance club called the Rockettes. Even started taking girls to the movies. I was so cool I always took them up to the balcony, the sophisticated place in those Negro movie houses in St. Louis. If the picture wasn't so good you could always smoke and hug your girl and make jokes.

The trick there was to go to the movie house before you picked up your girl and slip the usher some money to save you a couple of balcony seats. Then you'd come back with your girl and wink at the usher and say: "Hi, baby," and he'd take you right upstairs. Sometimes, the usher would be out to lunch and all the balcony seats would be filled. That was the worst feeling in the world. But usually you'd get up there, and when the movie was over you'd strut down from the balcony, real slow, so everyone could see how cool you were, how important. You knew somebody, you had connections. You never let anyone know you tipped the usher. In those days, all I really wanted out of life was always to be able to sit in the balcony.

That year, I was in the balcony all right, winning races, playing drums, going out. Everything went my way. Once there was a night track meet, and the lights went out in the middle of the race. I sneaked off across the field, taking a short cut, and fell over a hurdle. I was lying there when the lights went on again. The officials tried to disqualify me. Not a chance. I told them that any fool knows that when the power fails during a night athletic event, the race in progress is automatically canceled and then rerun. They looked at each other and coughed, and I guess they didn't know their own rules too well. I had just made that up on the spur of the moment. The race was rerun.

And then one day I decided I wanted to be president of my senior class. Only certain people had ever been class president: kids from high-class families who had perfect attendance records, were in the National Honor Society, belonged to the French Club and the Math Club and the service organizations. So I got my own organization. The hoodlums. I went around and talked to all those cats who used to stand outside the proms, all those guys who didn't have anything going for them and I told them I wanted this thing, that I was their representative. They went and they got it for me, they spread the word that if anybody else won the election he might as well quit. I was class president.

That was another turning point for me. A new feeling of responsibility for others. In track, I was running just for myself. But as president of the graduating class at Sumner High School I knew my shirt had to be clean, my shoes had to be polished, I couldn't cut class or come late or sit in the toilet and watch crap games or yell out crazy things in class. There were obligations, meetings to go to, a Senior Day speech to write. I had to talk to the white man who came through selling senior class rings for twenty dollars each. I had to work out how he would take his orders and collect his money and then give out the rings. I wasn't able to afford one myself.

I had never really thought about college until that last semester in high school when scholarship offers began coming in from colleges around the country. Momma had only finished the third grade, and so just finishing high school was a big dream in our family. College was for people with money. After high school you get yourself some kind of a job. There were more than one hundred offers, colleges from California to Massachusetts, but my grades were too low for most of the schools. I was probably the only class president in the country that year who was in the lowest fifth of more than 700 students. I tried to study that year, to read books, but I just didn't know how. At eight o'clock, after track practice, I'd sit down in the kitchen and try to read. God, I'm going to sit here until midnight if I have to, I'm going to read this book, even if it takes an hour to read every page, I'm going to sit here and read, one word at a time. And then the words started getting fuzzy and my mind started drifting, floating off to a million places.

Didn't matter, it was still my year. Coach St. James had gone to Southern Illinois University in Carbondale, and he said he could help me get in. He thought it would be the best school for me, a chance to be a big fish in a little pond. Southern Illinois wanted to give me an entrance exam, but I didn't even show up for it, I was so sure I would flunk. I talked to the coach down there and told him that if he wanted me to run track for him I wouldn't take any tests. He sent me to the dean, who made a deal: I could go to college, on an athletic-work scholarship, without taking the entrance exam. But the first quarter I made bad grades I'd have to take the exam and pass it, or leave school. Ironman Gregory won again.

Didn't have to study, didn't even have to train for my track meets any more. Wrapped my legs in tape and told the coach I hurt too much to practice. I stayed out late, went to dances, took girls up to the balcony, drank beer. Even bought a pack of cigarettes. I started letting the vice-president of the class go to the student government meetings. When the teachers kept asking me if my Senior Class Day speech was ready yet, I told them I was working on it. Tomorrow. It'll be ready tomorrow. I guess I thought I'd just go up there and tell jokes. I really thought I was great stuff, bigger than the Gregory family, bigger than the school, right up there with God. I remember the day we walked out to Forest Park for the final meet of my high school career, and all along the way there were papers on the newsstands with headlines that read: "Dick Gregory Closes Out One of Most Brilliant Careers in History of St. Louis H.S. Track." One headline even read: "Dick Gregory Wins State Meet Second Year in Row." Somebody must have lost his job on that one, because it rained when we got out to Forest Park and the meet was postponed.

All that week there were stories in the newspapers about how Dick Gregory was going to close out his high school career in style, in a blaze of glory. I believed every word. Didn't bother to train, stayed up late, made all the senior parties. Then we went out to Forest Park again and the sun was out and the press was there and the bands and the photographers and crowds were waiting for me to close out this brilliant high school career. It was a hell of a close-out all right. I finished seventeenth.

I couldn't believe it. Neither could anyone else. After the race I just hung around the finish line, waiting for them to disqualify the sixteen runners who finished ahead of me. The coach was mad and the press was disgusted and I was ashamed. The headlines didn't even mention who won the race, just: "Dick Gregory Finishes Disappointing 17th." I went back to school, and they started asking me about my speech again, and I just shrugged and walked away. I had gotten so big in my own mind that when I disappointed myself there was nothing left to fall back on. Too big for Momma, too big for the teachers, too big for God. But I was wrong again. The day before the senior ceremony, one of the English teachers handed me a speech.

I walked up on the stage that day and it seemed as though the whole world was holding its breath. When the principal pinned the school colors on me, his hand was shaking so much he stuck the pin right into my chest. I stepped behind the microphone. Suddenly I had that feeling again, the hot water flowing upward, the monster growing to crush the world, and that teacher's speech felt like it was mine.

"You know, since the beginning of time, man has used symbols . . ."

Suddenly, the whole goddamned auditorium stopped shifting and whispering, everyone froze, spellbound.

". . . the crude stone tablets, unearthed by archeologists, symbolized the feeble attempt of man to record his thoughts and his history . . ."

The teachers lost their terrified expressions, the students' mouths dropped open.

". . . the cross, so familiar in Christian civilization . . . the bald eagle . . . to many a symbol of democratic ideals . . ."

They were leaning toward me now, everybody, as if they wanted to run up and hug me.

". . . a symbol of man's efforts to live harmoniously with his fellow man. Today, we have gathered for a great symbolic experience. Colors Day. The maroon and white of Sumner High School, a symbol that for years has caused a little fire to burn in the hearts of many. Now we have joined this multitude. Needless to say, we will wear the maroon and white, this symbol of the years we have spent in learning and thought and growth, with justifiable pride in the years to come."

I was done and you could hear the breath rush out of hundreds of lungs, and then they started cheering and shouting and the hoodlums nearly tore the auditorium down and the teachers were smiling and shaking each other's hands and I looked down at Momma, and all I could see was tears in her eyes and she was moving her lips and I knew just what she looked like when she was alone and saying, Thank God, oh, thank God.

VII

I was walking down the main street of Carbondale, Illinois, in 1953 and a white man touched my arm.

"Dick Gregory?"

"Yeah, that's right."

"You don't know me, but my son and I always come to watch you run. He's sitting in the car over there, he can't walk without crutches. I'd be much obliged if you'd say hello to him and give him an autograph. It would mean a lot to him."

"Be glad to."

We walked over to the car and opened the front door. He was a skinny little boy, maybe nine years old.

"John, this is Dick Gregory. He wants to say hello to you."

I leaned in and shook his little hand. His legs were in heavy metal braces. "Real glad to meet you, John. Your Daddy tells me you're a big fan. You always come out to cheer for Southern. You know, we always run a lot faster when there's folks behind us."

The little boy smiled, very shyly, and pulled out a ten-cent-store album. "Would you sign my autograph book?"

"Sure, John. Got a pencil?"

John didn't have a pencil. Neither did his father. It was a Sunday, and the only place we could get a pencil was the restaurant we were standing in front of. I turned to the father.

"They'll give you a pencil in there."

He looked at me a little strangely, but he went in and got a pencil. He handed it to me as if he thought I should have walked into the restaurant and gotten the pencil myself. I signed the autograph book, told John I'd be looking for him in the stands next week, and walked away. Quickly. I could feel the father's eyes on my back, could hear him thinking about some uppity nigger making him go fetch a pencil. Somehow I didn't feel I could explain to him that Negroes weren't allowed in that restaurant, that before I could have asked for a pencil I would have heard that woman behind the cash register say, "I'm sorry, but you know we're not allowed to serve colored in here."

I don't know if that father and his little crippled son would have believed me. What the hell, Dick Gregory *owned* Carbondale. Captain of the cross-country team, captain of the track team, financial grant, busboy in the president's house, fastest half-miler in the school's history, drummer in the orchestra and the marching band, big actor in the variety show, Outstanding Athlete of 1953. The only things Dick Gregory couldn't do in Carbondale were eat out with his teammates and sit in the orchestra section of the movie house. I should have gotten that little crippled kid's autograph. He was an American.

Sometimes it seemed as though all the manhood I won for myself out on the track was taken away when I got into town. You run and you tear your body apart and you win and the crowd goes wild shouting your name and your teammates carry you off the field on their shoulders and Doc Lingle, the coach, throws his arms around you, and when the team goes off downtown for a steak and a beer you have to tell them you can't make it, you have something better to do. I didn't finish a single book while I was in college, but I learned a lot and I got myself an attitude.

In the beginning, I could fool myself. When I left for Southern Illinois in March of 1952 for the spring quarter with a metal suitcase and a shopping bag full of Momma's baloney sandwiches and a fried chicken, it was a thrill just to be going out of town. I had slipped out on the neighborhood; just Momma and me and some of the kids went down to the Greyhound Bus Terminal in St. Louis. And it was a bigger thrill when I got to Carbondale, left the shopping bag under my seat on the bus, and walked on the campus. I was in college, I was really in college. It was going to be beautiful.

I made the team right away, as a freshman, and I made a lot of friends. There were mostly white kids at school and white instructors, and not too many of them had heard of me. I had never seen so many white folks in one place before, except in parades and during election campaigns when they'd have Colored Day picnics and let the black babies pee all over them for the vote. But I wasn't too nervous because I had talked to white boys during track meets in high school. And I had my equalizer: I could always go out on the track and crush the world.

I developed as a runner. Leland P. Lingle was a fine coach and a fine man. He was the first white man to stretch out his hand to me. It was Doc Lingle who told me to take courses in Speech and Drama and Music. It was Doc Lingle who laughed at my jokes and said I'd be a first-rate entertainer some day. He was a kind man. He used to buy me a $1.25 steak dinner at the University Cafeteria every time I broke a school record, and he never complained when I purposely lowered the record a tenth of a second at a time just to get more steaks. I eventually brought the half-mile record down to 1 minute 54.1 seconds.

But I was still very confused. Track became something different for me in college. In high school I was fighting being broke and on relief, and each Saturday I'd go out and recharge my batteries, be a hero for another week. But in college I was fighting being Negro. That's not a temporary condition. It was a hell of a thing for me to be running good track in college and walk past a downtown restaurant and see a teammate in there eating a sandwich and drinking a malt with his girl. He'd look up and smile and wave at me through the plate-glass window. I'd wave back and I'd say to myself: "Eat up good, 'cause tomorrow I'm going to crush you on the track." But by the time tomorrow rolled around, I'd have swallowed the hurt down and I'd go out and show that guy how to shift his weight when he took the turn.

There were the weekends the team went traveling, and

we'd all be sitting in some roadside diner, and the only reason I was in there was because I was one of Doc Lingle's boys. Local white folks would walk in and look at me and nudge each other. I never talked about it with my white friends because it's not something you can tell them about. All you can do is sit in the team bus with your metal suitcase across your knees and bang on it like it was a drum and sing calypso songs and tell jokes. Happy-go-lucky Greg. Personality Kid. Funny man. Always laughing. Sure. Momma always said there was more hope in laughing.

There were quite a few Negroes at Southern, and we stuck together. Roomed together and dated and partied and hung around together. We'd walk downtown in twos and threes, and as we passed those restaurants the white kids would come out and say: "Where you going, Greg?" and I'd wink and say: "Got a little party to go on, Big Daddy." We hardly ever took our white friends down to the Negro neighborhood. They must have thought segregation worked both ways. That wasn't true. There were two honky-tonk bars down in the Negro section and we were a little too ashamed of them to bring our white friends down.

There were a lot of things I didn't tell the white boys, because I couldn't take the chance that they wouldn't understand. About Momma, and how she was in and out of the hospital these days, the diabetes and the heart trouble getting worse, a bad-smelling discharge coming out of her that Dolores thought was cancer. How could I explain how I felt about my Momma, and that as much as I loved her I didn't want to go back home? How could I explain that I was dying a slow death, too, in college, trying to figure out why I was running and going to business administration classes and working as a busboy in the president's dining room and planning my steps so I'd always be near the University Cafeteria or University Drug when I got hungry? How could I explain how I felt the day a white History instructor wrote the word Negro on the blackboard and spelled it with a small *n?* At the end of the hour I went to the

board and erased the letter and wrote in a capital *N*
Everybody stared and nobody said anything about it. I
don't know how long it all would have gone on, or what
I would have done if it hadn't been for what happened
in the movies.

I always liked the movie house in Carbondale. I
thought it was the coolest place in the world. In St.
Louis, it was always a big deal to get up into the balcony, but in Carbondale we had it made. As soon as I
got there, I found out that all the Negro athletes sat up
in the balcony. A bunch of us would go to the movies together, and we'd march right up to the balcony, and
laugh and make jokes about the picture. I always figured
that one of the juniors or seniors had taken care of the
usher. I remembered the first time I went to the movies
alone, I bought a ticket with my last penny, and I just
sort of stood around downstairs, looking for someone to
borrow a quarter from so I could tip the usher. I was
a little embarrassed when the usher, a white student I
had seen around campus, came up to me. I had nothing
for him.

"You're Dick Gregory, aren't you?"

"That's right."

He smiled at me. "We always hear a lot about you.
Nice to have you here. You can go right on upstairs,
there are plenty of seats."

Did I feel big. Didn't even have to tip the usher to get
up to the balcony any more. I knew someone, I had connections. "Thanks, baby, I'll take care of you next time,"
I told the usher.

The next time, I took a girl. I had promised to take
another girl to the movies that night, but at the last
minute I got another date. I was so afraid of running into
that first girl up in the balcony that I took my date and
sat downstairs. She jerked away from me and started
toward the stairs, but I grabbed her hand. "Come on,
baby, you're with me tonight."

She must have thought I meant that Dick Gregory was
such a big man he could go anywhere he wanted. She
seemed to be trembling when we sat downstairs but I

was so busy worrying about meeting that other girl that I didn't notice right away. Then I thought she was chilly. And I thought all the people downstairs turning and staring and pointing at us were whispering about that great track star, Dick Gregory. Then the usher came over.

"There are plenty of seats in the balcony, Greg."

"That's okay, baby, I'll sit here tonight."

"Greg, I'm sorry, but you have to go upstairs."

I figured that he wanted a tip from last time after all, so I started to lean over and explain why I couldn't take a chance on being seen up in the balcony tonight.

His voice got hard. "I said you have to go upstairs."

I still thought he was playing until he came back with the manager. "May I see you for a moment, Mister Gregory?" When white folks call you mister you know something is wrong.

I told the girl I'd be right back, never knowing I was leaving her down there with all that hell, the white folks downstairs turning and hissing and grumbling, and the Negroes upstairs cheering, yelling, "Go, baby, go, you give it to 'em, Greg." Until I got into the manager's office, I thought the balcony was cheering me for last week's race.

"I'm sorry, Mister Gregory, but you know you can't sit in the orchestra."

"Why not?"

"Because colored seating is in the balcony."

My St. Louis dream died that night, my dream about always being able to afford the balcony. In Carbondale, the balcony was my place. I stood there, so confused, wondering if the usher back home in St. Louis had been cheating me all those years, or if this man was trying to destroy something I had.

"If you want me in the balcony, you'll have to put me there."

"Do you want me to call the police?"

"Go ahead."

He called the police. I almost laughed. How many times had I given an usher a tip to save me a balcony seat and when I got there the usher was gone and the balcony was full and *I* wanted to call the police. Now, here's a man calling a cop to get me up to the balcony.

I went back and got my date and left. She was crying. On the way out, the manager said: "Be sure and get your money back."

"Keep it. I'll be back."

I went back alone the next night and sat downstairs. They gave me the okay. Let him sit downstairs, he's crazy, anybody who bucks this system is crazy and we don't punish insane people here in America. And the nights after that I started bringing Negro friends, guys who weren't Dick Gregory, big athlete, guys who couldn't be crazy. If I had thought about it, I should have brought Doc Lingle or the dean or the president of the University.

And then Hollywood produced that great movie about Jesus Christ called *The Robe*. The movie house in Carbondale had paid a lot of money for that movie, and one night, while I was sitting downstairs, the manager invited me to his office. He was scared to death. He told me how much money he had spent for the picture, how afraid he was of going bankrupt, how he couldn't afford to lose white customers at a time like this. If I promised not to sit downstairs while *The Robe* was showing, everything would be all right afterwards. Negroes could sit anywhere they wanted to. I was sick and tired of negotiating for my rights. I agreed.

I was sitting in that movie house—in the balcony—on the night that Momma died. It was a good thing I was in the balcony that night because Doc Lingle would never have thought to look for me downstairs. He called me out into the aisle, and told me to telephone home.

"Is it Momma, Doc?"

"Just call home, Dick."

"Is she dead?"

"Just call home."

"Doc?"

"I'm very sorry, Dick."

When I finally got through on the phone, Dolores said: "Hurry home, Richard. Momma is dead."

"No need to rush now, 'Lores."

I went back to my room and started to pack and my roommate said: "Think nice thoughts about her, Greg, how much good she did and how much pain she was in. Make you feel better."

I cried and I prayed that night, thinking of Momma and blaming myself. If I hadn't gone to college, if I had stayed home and gotten a job, Momma wouldn't have had to keep on working in white folks' houses, riding the streetcar with basket lunches to sell to the colored porters in the downtown hotels, hiding the telephone when the relief worker came around. My Momma was forty-eight years old when she died.

I took the bus home the next morning. I couldn't believe I was sitting in the house on North Taylor again and Momma wasn't coming home. I jumped up every time the streetcar stopped, and suddenly I realized why I always stayed out and played until night. When Momma wasn't there it wasn't a home; it was nothing but a house. I didn't have too much to say to my brothers and sisters. After we talked about Momma, we just sat around, not looking at each other. I wandered around the neighborhood, just to hear Missis Simmons and Missis Rector and Mister Ben talk about what a great woman she was. I thought maybe Big Pres would show up. She would have come back from the dead for that.

Momma lay at the undertaker's with a smile on her face, wearing all those fine, rich white folks' clothes. She finally had a place to wear them. I bent over and kissed her and said: Thanks, Momma, some day I'm going to do something to make you proud of me. And I walked out and a voice in my head said: You'll be all right, Richard, just be careful, wrap up good, and don't wear tight belts against that poor stomach of yours. Everybody wondered why I didn't cry. It hurt too much to cry.

At the funeral the next day I stood away from everybody else while those dirty little men in muddy overalls leaned on their rusty shovels and smoked while the preacher read. I wanted to run up to them and pull their shovels away and tell them not to throw dirt in my Momma's face, but all her white folks had come to the cemetery and I knew Momma didn't want me to mess up in front of all her good white folks. So they threw the dirt in her face and I turned and walked back to the house and packed. I knew it would be the last time I'd ever be in that house because it wasn't my home any more. I went out to the backyard and looked up at the sky and said: I'm sorry, Momma, sorry I was embarrassed because we were on relief, sorry I was ashamed of you because you weren't dressed the way other kids' mothers were dressed, sorry you had to die before I realized what a great lady you were.

VIII

I went back to school numb and I stayed that way for most of the next four years, through the rest of that year at school, through two years in the Army, through the last year at college. It wasn't a sleepy numbness; it was a cold, hard, bitter numbness. It got me the Outstanding Athlete Award of 1953.

I remember the day I walked past the Athletic Department office, a few weeks after Momma died, and for the first time I really noticed the pictures along the walls. There were rows and rows of Negro athletes' pictures, but along the top of the wall, where the pictures of each year's Outstanding Athlete hung, there were only white faces. A school eighty-four years old and not one Negro had ever won the award. It was time.

So I walked up to the coach and told him that if I wasn't elected Outstanding Athlete for 1953, I was going to quit. I threatened them so cool that they couldn't even give it to another Negro—I went to them as an individual, made them think it had to do with me, not race. I made it. Outstanding Athlete of the Year, and all I could do was run track; never picked up a basketball, couldn't play baseball, didn't know how to swim. The next year another Negro, Leo Wilson, made it, and we've been making it ever since. But someone had to break the ice—with a threat. I remember that night in June they gave out the award at a big dinner, and when they handed it to me I thanked them and then I said to myself: Thanks, Greg, you got it for yourself, the same way you got to be class president in high school. A sports commentator flew down from St. Louis to do a thirty-minute show on Dick Gregory, greatest athlete ever to

87

hit Southern Illinois University. A St. Louis boy. And would you believe it, he was born on relief?

I never got to be as good a runner as Doc Lingle and the newspapers said I would. Too busy playing around, getting my attitude. I started doing some satire then. I didn't know it was satire. It was just standing on a stage during the all-fraternity variety show and talking to a crowd of white people about school and athletics and the world situation and how tough it was to run away from home these days unless you came from a family with a second car. For a while, standing on that stage and watching those people laugh with me, I thought it was even better than winning a track meet. But running track was safer: You can be saying the funniest things in the world but if Whitey is mad at you and has hate, he might not laugh. If you're in good condition and you can run faster than Whitey, he can hate all he wants and you'll still come out the better man.

My last big thrill in track was qualifying for the National Collegiate Meet for small colleges, in Texas. I was rated third in the nation in the half-mile for a little while, and I was proud and scared to be able to run with the best boys, white and black, from all over the country. I stood on that field on the opening day of the meet and it was like the best of all the Thanksgivings and Christmases, listening to the marching band play "The Star-Spangled Banner," and seeing the flag snap in the wind, and knowing that it was all for me, too. It was like all the war movies I had seen back in St. Louis and in Carbondale, pulling for the American soldiers, cheering for the good guys, feeling a part of something so big and strong and fine. I was beaten in the preliminaries of that meet, but I was proud just to have been there. And then I went back to school and it was like coming out of that movie, suddenly realizing there weren't any Negro soldiers in that picture, "I'm sorry but you know we're not allowed to serve colored in here." All the joy and inspiration of being an American was gone.

When you're a little kid you can press your nose against a plate-glass window and tell yourself you are going to grow up some day and be able to go inside. You can tell yourself you are going to grow up some day and be a man, and do all the things a man can do. These are nice dreams for kids. But when you walk down the street and see your track team friends on the other side of that plate-glass window, where you can't go, you can't even tell yourself to wait until you grow up. You are already a man, and knowing that there is no dream just strips your manhood away and brings you all the way back down to the gutter.

It's a hard thing to be a big athlete on campus and to go downtown and feel like the chump who dropped the ball on Homecoming Day, to walk down a street and have farmers and little kids wave and call to you like you're a big man and know in your heart that every one of them is really bigger than you. There was a man in Carbondale, a white man who owned a clothing store, and I used to borrow money at school so I could go in there and buy socks and ties I didn't even need, just so I could walk around that section of town and have some place to go. He was a kind man, and we talked about history and about sports and he even gave me credit. But he wasn't enough to keep me from wondering about people who didn't break down those segregation laws, who didn't check on teachers who spelled Negro with a small *n,* who didn't build dorms for the Negro coeds so they didn't have to live in Negro roominghouses two miles from campus in a town without buses. Sure, the Negro men lived in the dorms, but that was because so many of us were gladiators. We had to be watched. And I wondered how we Negroes were able to sit in the stands and cheer for Southern Illinois to win a football game against a team that had more Negroes than ours did. Of course, every time a Negro got the ball, on either team, we hoped he went for a touchdown. We sat together in the stands, because when you're mixed in with the whites you hear a guy behind you say: "Look at that nigger go," and then a white tackler dives at the Negro runner and the Negro shakes him loose and goes all the way for the touchdown and you want to turn around and say: "Go ahead, call him another nigger." But you don't.

You hang around and drift around and don't even bother with your student deferment. I was drafted in 1954 and I didn't care much what happened to me in the Army. I'd sleep in my bunk all day, I'd fall out to formation wearing blue suède shoes, I'd salute with my left hand. When I was on K.P. I'd crawl into a big pot and go to sleep, and when the mess sergeant started banging on the pot I'd refuse to come out unless he paid me the minimum hourly wage. A colonel came by one day on inspection and asked me what I was doing in the pot.

"We ran out of chipped beef, sergeant," I said to the colonel, "and I volunteered to be cooked for lunch."

The next day, I was brought to the colonel's office. I walked in without saluting and sat down without permission. He just shook his head.

"Gregory," he said, leaning across his desk, "you are either a great comedian or a goddamned malingerer. There is an open talent show at the service club tonight. You will go down there, and you will win it. Otherwise, I will court-martial you. Now get the hell out of here."

I won it. I just stood up there and talked about the system and the Army and the post and the officers. I told them how the Army charged me eighty-five dollars when I lost my rifle. That's why in the Navy the captain always goes down with his ship. And I won the next talent show, and the one after that, and the next thing I knew I was in Special Services on an Army tour.

I kept running, too. On the athletic field I met Jim Ellis, who became one of my best friends. Jim was a big, handsome lieutenant who had been All-America at Michigan State. He was an All-Army halfback. He used to lend me an extra officer's uniform and let me sleep in the bachelor officers' quarters. We used to tear around Fort Lee together in his car. We balled it up pretty good, and whenever we ran out of money I'd call Doc Lingle, collect, sometimes in the middle of the night. Somehow, Doc always came through.

I started developing little routines now, in between

clowning around and playing the bongos and singing a few calypso songs. I worked at a little Negro club in Petersburg, Virginia. I'd come onstage wearing long white underwear, a big black cowboy hat, and a painted mustache and sideburns. Once I got the audience's attention, I could start talking, tell them about my home in St. Louis, so cold the snow wouldn't melt on the floor, the bed so crowded we had to leave bookmarks to save our place when we got up to go to the toilet in the middle of the night. I never really prepared for those shows, or for the Army shows. In 1955 I qualified for the All-Army Show at Fort Dix, New Jersey. The winners from that show would go on Ed Sullivan's television show. I didn't make it, probably the best thing that could have happened. I would have been destroyed if I had made the Sullivan show in 1955, knowing nothing about show business, being on there by accident. I would have had the wrong attitude. I probably would never have worked as hard as I did later. But I was disappointed then, and kind of hung up when I got out of the Army in the spring of 1956. No place to go. Nothing much to do. The day I cleared post I had to fill out a form with my home address on it. I wrote Southern Illinois University, Carbondale, Illinois. It seemed like the only home I had, so I decided then to go back.

It was different back at school now. There was a new athletic system, putting more emphasis on football, shoving Doc Lingle off in a corner. I got back on the track team, but I wasn't really interested, couldn't figure out what I was running for. I stayed through summer school, on into the fall quarter, and my grades were poor. I tell people I was flunking out because it's simpler than explaining that there just wasn't any more reason to stay. Most of my friends were gone, and in the fall we got a collection called "Dimes for Doc," to send the coach to the Olympic Games in Helsinki. Doc left, and I decided I might as well go, too.

Once I would have been afraid to go out into that white man's world without my diploma, but now I knew that it really didn't matter. I'd been around. I'd seen Negroes who had been graduated from white man's colleges with that piece of white paper driving cabs and carrying mail. I'd seen Negroes who got all A's in accounting go downtown to the big department stores only to hear, "Sorry, we're not hiring porters today." That piece of white paper isn't enough unless they graduate you with a white face, too.

Then the old monster jumped me again. It wasn't going to let me tuck down my head and crawl out of Carbondale. So I sent myself a telegram.

I was laying around my dorm room when the telegram came. Was I cool. Never got a telegram before, but I just lay there as if I got one every day. My roommate got all excited.

"Aren't you going to open it, Greg?"

"Read it to me, baby."

I knew the message by heart. COME TO BALTIMORE MARYLAND IMMEDIATELY GUARANTEE $25,000 A YEAR START SIGNED FRANK D'ALESANDRO.

"Is this a gag, Greg?"

"Nope. I was in the Army with Frank. His Daddy's mayor of Baltimore. Said he could get me a job in show business anytime I wanted. Think I should take it?"

He ran out of that room, waving that telegram, screaming up and down the halls of the dorm. Nobody ever bothered to see that the telegram had been filed at the Carbondale office. They all came in to congratulate me. The whole campus flipped. For two days I walked around, showing that telegram to everybody who could read, from the president of the University to the guys who cleaned up the stadium. The dean of students read it, and we talked, and he said that maybe I should go. He put his arm around my shoulders, and we looked out his window at where they were breaking ground for the new Student Union. I had led the campaign for the new Union, and now I'd never see it built.

"Dick, you've been more than a student here. You've been a living part of this school. Southern Illinois University has taken personality from you, and you've taken personality from Southern Illinois.'

The kids threw me a farewell party, and everybody wished me good luck. I tried to feel ashamed, but I couldn't. I was only lying to them for a little while. I'd make it big somehow, somewhere. Some day that $25,000 telegram would come true.

That night I went down to the Greyhound Bus terminal and bought a ticket to Chicago. My brother Presley was working in Chicago at that time, and I figured he could help me get a job. I told the kids who came to see me off that I had me a little girl in Chicago, and I was going to have me a little ball before I took a direct flight to Baltimore and settled down to show business. I waved to them through the bus window, and suddenly the monster drained right out of me and I felt like I was leaving the whole world behind, leaving everybody who would ever say: "There goes Dick Gregory." I made the bus driver stop, and I got my bags off, and I ran back to campus, crying all the way.

Back at the dorms I saw all those happy faces who believed in me, all those people who wanted to shake my hand again and wish me good luck again. I had to live up to them. They had said their good-bys, they had sent me off like a champ, and now I had to go. I made up some story about not wanting to ride a bus now that I was almost a star, and I borrowed some money. The kids took me down to the train station.

A night train can be the loneliest place in the world when you look out the window and all you see is darkness moving fast. I showed my telegram to the porter.

"You do a good job, son," he said. "They'll all be watching you. Show them what we can do."

I tipped him all the money I had left, just for believing me.

" . . . and they didn't even have what I wanted."

I

I'm driving through a snowstorm on an empty gas tank and my girl friend's mother wants Scotch. My girl friend's brothers and sisters are hollering for food. And I'm figuring like mad. Got five dollars. It's supposed to be dollar night at the drive-in movie, which leaves me four dollars to grandstand with. Plenty for hot dogs. But a bottle of Scotch can wipe me out. It's their car, and if they want a tankful of gas out of me, that'll wipe me out, too. But if I take a chance, and we run dry and I have to call a cab . . .

"We better stop and get some gas, Dick," says Maryann's mother.

"You're so right, I'm looking for a station now," I say, passing one on each side of the road.

Every traffic light winks at me as if to say, "If you're lucky, you'll get arrested." I jump every light, but nothing happens. Never find a cop when you want one.

"Gas station, there's a gas station," yells one of the four little kids in the back.

I pull in alongside the pump and lean out. "Fill her up, baby."

Then I jump out of the car and run to the back. "Just one dollar's worth, please."

Through the window I can see Maryann's mother talking away at her daughter in the front of the car. The four little kids are rubbing their hungry bellies in the back seat. They are all very impressed to be going out with such a big entertainer. Dick Gregory, master of ceremonies and star comic of the Esquire Show Lounge of Chicago, buys his suits at Lytton's and has his own apartment.

I get back into the car looking very put out.

"What's wrong, Dick?"

"Hell, I didn't like that man's attitude. I never spend my money with a man whose attitude I don't like."

"You're so right," says the mother. "Why I was telling Maryann only yesterday that . . ."

Now if I can get Maryann off alone and explain the situation to her I'm all right. I don't have to be phony with her. Of course, it would never dawn on me to embarrass the girl in front of her folks. Besides, people just don't like to know that such a big entertainer makes thirty dollars a week, buys his clothes on the credit of a landlady who works nights at a drugstore, and rents a basement room.

"Sure is cold," says the mother.

"We're almost there, get us some good hot coffee."

"Some Scotch would warm us much faster, Dick."

"Liquor store, there's a liquor store," yells a kid.

Like God strung it down from heaven, right across the highway, is this big sign: LAST LIQUOR STORE BEFORE DRIVE-IN. Even I can't miss it, and I'm trying.

I pull over and get out. I've never bought whiskey before. I walk right up to the guy behind the counter.

Then, out of the corner of my eye, I see the sign: SPECIAL ON SCOTCH—$1.25 A PINT. I'm saved. Maryann and I won't drink. Her mother can have the whole pint. I run back to the car.

"Didn't they have any cups, Dick?" asks Maryann's mother.

Things are very tight now. Got two dollars and fifty cents, and something tells me I read the newspaper wrong, just my luck it's not dollar night after all. By the time we pull up to the box office I'm in a cold sweat despite the freezing weather. I'm sure it's not dollar night.

"That will be one dollar, mister."

"What the hell you mean, the paper said one dollar."

"That's just what I said, mister, one dollar."

Now I'm scared again. The only other time I'd been

to a drive-in movie was two years ago, in college. How did the driver do it? Where do you park? Where do you get the speaker and the heater?"

"We're holding up traffic, Dick."

It's no trouble at all, and I'm so thankful I give the kids the rest of the money to buy hot dogs and soda. My stomach is turning over, and my hands are still shaking, and thank God everybody's quiet now, watching the movie, and I can close my eyes and figure out how I got here in the first place.

It had been a short trip, that train ride from Carbondale to Chicago, but some of the days that followed were very long. Presley had left his roominghouse, with no forwarding address, but his landlady let me stay there for a few days, until I got a Christmas job at the Post Office and a hotel room. I kept flipping the letters to Mississippi in the foreign slot, but I held the job until January. I hadn't made any friends in Chicago and I couldn't get another job. I was on my way back to the train station, with no destination in mind, when I ran into a guy I had run track with back in high school. I remember standing on a windy corner, getting colder and colder, just talking to keep from going to that station. I told the guy about college, about the Army, about Lieutenant Jim Ellis. . . .

"You mean Tank Ellis, the football player?" said the guy. "Man, I was over his house last night on a party."

"Where's he live?"

"Fifty-one oh three Wabash."

I started running.

When Jim Ellis' door opened, things began to open up for me in Chicago. He treated me like a long-lost brother and he got me a job with him out at Ford Aircraft. After work, we'd go to the park together and run to get him in condition for the pro football tryouts in the spring. I ran and I ran and it felt good as that old machine started to get into shape. I was beating Jim every day. He wasn't a track man, but it's a nice feeling to beat an All-American. Jim had a fast, hip crowd that threw a lot of parties, and I was swinging with people that liked me and my jokes. When Jim left for summer camp, I started running with the University of Chicago track team and made more friends, like Herbert Jubert and Ira Murchison. Murch was the fastest 100-yard-dash man in the world and had records to prove it. I started seeing Presley, who was a door-to-door salesman, and Ron, my youngest brother, who was a track star at the University of Notre Dame. And in September I moved in with Ozelle and William Underwood, a young couple who had a basement room to rent. They treated me like a member of the family. I lost the Ford job in October, but it wasn't so bad. Whenever I was depressed, I could put on that track suit and run. After a while, I fell into the habit I had in high school—running early in the morning and at night when people were going and coming from work. I wanted to be seen.

I had a good Christmas with the Underwoods that year, and I was able to call St. Louis and tell Dolores and Garland and Pauline I was doing all right, and take the train to visit Ron in South Bend. But then January came and I was still out of work, and there was something about unemployment compensation that began to remind me of relief: The way they made you stand in line, the way they narrowed their eyes when they asked questions. I was getting more and more depressed, and there seemed to be less and less time to run it out of my system. I wasn't doing anything. I wasn't getting anywhere. And then, on a Saturday night in late January, I hooked up with the monster again. In a night club.

Ozelle and William were having some people over that night and I slipped out early. I didn't feel social. I caught a double-feature, and just started walking, up streets I didn't remember, into a South Side neighborhood I had never seen before. There was a little neighborhood night club on a corner, jukebox and entertainment on the weekends. The place was packed with Saturday-night faces, happy faces. I walked in. The master of ceremonies was the comic, and his material was blue and old, but after a while I was laughing too, and I had forgotten the reason I was out that night. After the show, I went backstage and told the man how much I had enjoyed his routine. We started talking, and I told him I was a comedian, too. I gave him my last five dollars, and he let me follow his act on the next show.

"Got a man here that's supposed to be funny," he said to the crowd. "Let's bring him on and find out."

I went out there scared, and I wasn't funny at first. I started talking and creating and I don't remember what I said, but after a while I was getting respectful laughs. The M.C. came out and took the microphone back. "You're a real funny man," he said. "You'll go far in show business."

I wasn't sure then if he was being sarcastic or not, but I figured I had done pretty well getting even weak laughs on clean material after following his blue jokes.

The next Saturday night I went to another Negro night club, the Esquire Show Lounge. I slipped Flash Evans, the M.C., five dollars, and this time I got a nice introduction and I followed the band's first set. I gave a masterpiece of a show that night. I just felt right and cool, and the crowd had come to laugh.

I never let them stop laughing, hit them hard and fast with jokes on processed hair and outer space and marijuana and integration and the numbers racket and long white Cadillacs and The Man downtown, and my dumb cousin and my mother-in-law, and the world situation. By the time I stopped my handkerchief was soaked and I had run out of cigarettes and I felt like I had passed them all, snatched them off like weeds, and broken the tape. When I came offstage the owner of the Esquire took me in a corner. The cheap son-of-a-bitch let me buy myself a drink, and asked me if I'd like to start as M.C. in two weeks. Friday Saturday, and Sunday. Ten dollars a night. I sat there and I looked at that man and I couldn't believe him. He said it again. I didn't know how I was going to wait until my opening night.

It came, finally, and I wasn't funny at all. It's one thing to be funny when you're a guest on another man's stage, something else again when it's your stage and you have to be funny night after night. My training began, now, but it was beautiful because the people in the Esquire were like a new family, the customers in the Esquire were like the student body when I was president of the class, and the women looked up to me as the big entertainer. For a girl like Maryann, I was the biggest entertainer she knew.

"Dick, wake up now, the movie's over."

"Wasn't sleeping, baby." I'm not about to tell her her I was starring in a little movie of my own.

I start the car and slip it into gear and the tires just whine. We don't move. First, second, reverse, first again. We're stuck in the snow. I get out of the car and walk around it. The back tires have spun themselves deep into the ice and slush. A lot of other cars at the drive-in are stuck, too. Seven white boys, mean-looking cats in jeans and boots and black leather jackets with a million zippers, are pushing the cars out, I watch them. They swagger up to a car whose tires are spinning and one of them says, "Okay, mister, you're next. Five bucks." They get their five, and they all get around the car and push it out toward the gate. Then they turn to another car. If the first car gets stuck again before it gets out on the highway, the seven cats will push it again—for another five. I don't even have a dime. I get back into the car.

"We're hungry," say the little kids in the back. I have to get them home quick. The tires whine some more.

"Okay, mister, you're next. Five bucks."

"Thanks anyway," I say, "I think I can get it out myself."

The windshield is steamed up, and the tires spin and whine some more.

"It's getting awfully cold, Dick," says Maryann's mother. "Why don't you let those boys push us out?"

"I regard this as a personal challenge, man over the forces of nature," I tell her.

"We hungry," say the kids.

"Man must triumph over nature. I must get this car out myself or perish in the attempt," I say.

"But it's only snow," says Maryann's mother.

"Yeah, but it's *white* snow," I say. A very good line, but no one laughs. The tires keep spinning.

"Well, you're ruining the tires," says Maryann's mother, angry now.

Then I get out of the car, and I walk over to the seven white cats with all their zippers. I might as well be a fool out here than in that car. I just look at them, and I say: "How in the world can you start out right and end up wrong? I'm not trying to steal anything and I'm not trying to do anything shady, but this is what happened. . . ."

And they stand there quietly in the snow, around me in a circle, and people are shouting and honking their horns and waving money. I explain the whole thing to them, I tell them the whole story about my girl's car and her mother and the gasoline and the Scotch and the hot dogs and dollar day, and they look at each other and nod their heads and the biggest of those cats says: "Get back in your car, mister, and roll down your windows so we can get a grip."

And I am almost crying as they are pushing, pushing for a friend, a hundred yards, then another hundred yards, out of the spin holes and past the box office and out the gate and they wave as I drive onto the highway and I lean out and yell: "Thanks, baby," like I just laid fifty dollars apiece on them. And now I'm driving down the highway and I look down on my lap and there's a five-dollar bill there that one of those beautiful cats slipped through the open window while he was pushing the car.

"We better get some gas," I say to Maryann's mother. "How much you want?"

"Just enough to get home on."

I'm smiling and laughing and crying and telling jokes as

I pull alongside that beautiful pump, and when the attendant runs out I just turn my head and say: "Fill 'er up, baby, all the way up, and don't forget to check the oil."

II

The Esquire Show Lounge is a big, rectangular room attached to a neighborhood bar on the South Side of Chicago. The room has chrome luncheonette-type tables, and chairs with red plastic seats. The customers buy bottles at the bar and get glasses and paper buckets filled with ice and cherries at their tables. There are red lights around the room, faded murals on the walls, and entertainment on the weekend: an M.C., a four-piece band, a shake dancer, some amateur talent now and then, and Guitar Red, an albino Negro who gets more out of an electric guitar than any man has a right to. He even plays with his feet. People come from all over Chicago to hear Guitar Red, and on Saturday nights there were lines around the block. But I was master of ceremonies and I introduced the acts and you had to get past me before you could see Guitar Red. I felt it was my show. And I felt like the Esquire Show Lounge was my home and my stadium.

All week long I would train for that Friday night show that started my weekend. For the first time since high school, I got that thirsty taste again, waiting each week to go out and crush the world. Only now I didn't have to beat anybody, I had to make people happy. Every day during the week I'd be working out for that three-day meet: buying comedy records, buying joke books, watching television, listening to people, going to the library and digging into musty old books of humor, and finding out where those comedy records got *their* material from. I walked downtown and spent money for books and magazines I couldn't even afford, and along the way I'd hang out in the Walgreen's at Sixty-third and Cottage

Grove and on corners and anywhere people were, listening to them talk, trying out thoughts and ideas and jokes on strangers. Ozelle and William would stay up half the night listening to new routines, and Ira Murchison and Herb Jubert and Jim Ellis would tell me what they liked and what they thought should go. I'd go to parties and just talk and create and clown and if something got a good response I'd mark it down in the back of my mind.

Morning, noon, and night, twenty-four hours a day, trying to develop a mind like I once developed a body, watching, listening, talking. Hours and hours of television, the "Ed Sullivan Show," the "Jack Paar Show," every comedy show, even funny old movies, and then the news shows, the soap operas, the westerns, the series. What makes people laugh, what are people thinking about?

And then you watch the stars, how do they act, how do they dress? I went down to Lytton's, a big department store in the Loop, and convinced them I was making a hundred dollars a week and had been working for four years. Ozelle and William helped me get clothes on credit. New shoes, new suits, new shirts. Change everything between shows. For the regular customers, you're the biggest entertainer they know. You have to look it. Keeping my clothes clean and buying records and books cost me as much as I was making. But I was selling a talent that wasn't really mine yet, and I had to develop it from every angle. I was hung up in something, and I had to find out how it worked.

Now people were beginning to say: "There goes Dick Gregory," again, and it was greater than track ever was because it was all for me; it didn't include the mothers' sons who had to lose so I could win. Between my shows I'd talk to people and sit at tables and walk around and shake hands. I met a lot of girls and I started going around with some of them. And I made rules for myself. Never go to a man's table if you think the woman with him is giving you the eye. That man is paying your salary—not much but he doesn't know that—and he deserves respect. He has the right to feel comfortable with his lady in the club. Never pick up the money that's

thrown onstage. There were nights when there was more
money on that stage than I was making in a week, but
I'd never let anyone know I needed that money. I was
the big entertainer. Never let a man pay me to introduce
him and his party from the floor. If he knew I'd take
that kind of money he couldn't respect me.

It's a wild thing about a small night club with ordinary,
working-class people. You can get the same kind of
respect there that you can get in the big, downtown
night club. You're those people's entertainer, the biggest
one they know, probably the biggest they will ever know.
The stars on the top have created such an atmosphere of
glamour that even the entertainers on the bottom can
step in and get respect. That's why you have to knock
yourself out to dress well and act right and keep yourself up. You can never say: Look here, I'm just a small-
time entertainer and my suits don't have to be pressed
or my act too sharp or my manners right. Where you
are, you're just as big as Milton Berle and Bob Hope
and Sammy Davis and Nipsey Russell. You're the big
big fish in the little little pond.

One Sunday, after my afternoon show, a girl came out
of the audience and asked me to come back to her table
and give some autographs. She said she'd like me to meet
her sisters. I told her I'd be delighted. That's why it's
so important to be nice and polite to people. You can
never tell when you're going to meet your future wife.

I walked over and there was a young girl at the table,
very bashful, very excited. She was twisting her napkin
to death, and giggling out of embarrassment. When I
sat down it was like God came over to the table. She
had never been in a night club before. She was from
Willard, Ohio, a small town, and her name was Lillian
Smith. She was a secretary over at the University of Chicago.

"You're fooling me, baby, you're really working at the
University?"

"No, I mean yes, I'm not fooling you."

"Well, look, Lillian, I'm over there nearly every day
to run track. Let's have lunch one day."

She tucked her head down and started giggling and she said: "Oh, no, you don't really mean that."

"Tell you what, Lillian, give me your phone number. I'll call you and tell you exactly what day we'll have lunch."

She was so nervous while she was writing it down, she kept tearing the paper with her pencil point. I rolled up the paper and put it in my pocket. Lillian Smith stayed through the second show and the Sunday evening show and she kept staring at me like she was afraid nobody in Willard, Ohio, would ever believe she had actually talked to this great man. When I left that night with the girl I was dating at the time, I went over and said good night to Lillian. I thought it might give her a thrill to call her, just because she was so sure I wouldn't.

That night, back at Ozelle and William's I lay in bed and thought about that face staring up at me, that soft, little-girl face so out of place in a night club. It suddenly dawned on me that my mother would have looked that way if she had ever been to a night club. I had a dream that night about Momma, and I was Richard again, and she came off the streetcar and ran into the house and said: "Richard, oh, Richard, I spoke to the star of the show, Harry Belafonte, I talked to Harry Belafonte," and I said: "No, Momma," and she said: "Yes, I did, I really did, and he's going to call me on the phone." When I woke up that Monday morning I called Lillian and I could almost see her expression over the phone. I just talked to her, and told her I'd call her back soon and we'd have lunch.

That was around the middle of April in 1958, and I only saw Lillian a few times. She was so bashful and shy, sometimes I just ran out of words. But I was getting better and better at the Esquire. I worked harder, got to be a night owl so I could go to the bars and restaurants where other show people hung out when they were finished working. I couldn't afford to watch them work, but I could always buy coffee or a drink and talk to them and listen. I used to walk into those places where nobody knew me, and I used to tell myself that some day I'd walk in there and everybody would turn around and say "Hi, Greg."

They knew me at the Esquire, though, my crowd. People were beginning to come to see me, not just for Guitar Red or Paul Bascomb's band or the shake dancer. I'd M.C. the show, and then I'd play bongos with Paul's band, then give my act, and M.C. the show some more, watching the time, keeping things moving like the patrol boy, like the president of the senior class. I'd go out to the show folks' after-work spots, get some sleep, spend the days working on my material, reading, listening, trying my routines on anybody who would sit still. I guess it got to be too much, because in the summer I came down with yellow jaundice. The day I went to the hospital, I called Lillian at her job. She was very concerned and very sweet, even though I hadn't talked to her in more than a month. It was like calling Momma.

I was in the hospital for six weeks, impatient and angry at missing all those weekends at the Esquire, but it was the first time I ever really slowed down enough to look back down the road, and up ahead. I thought about track and I thought about Doc Lingle, how he used to tell me to take Speech and Music to prepare for a career in show business. He knew. And that old lady who had seen a star in the middle of my head. She knew, too. I was going to go all the way.

There were a lot of visitors at the hospital—friends, performers, and customers from the Esquire. Girls. A lot of noise, a lot of talking. When the room finally would clear out, there was Lillian, standing shyly in the corner. The first time she came she brought me candy bars and grapes. You're not supposed to bring things into a Veterans Administration hospital, but I knew Lillian hadn't sneaked that paper bag past the desk. Some people can just walk into a place and never be stopped and never be questioned. She would stand there, her eyes full of concern, and we hardly talked because she was so shy and I couldn't always find things to say to her. When visiting hours were over the first

time, she asked if she could come back. I said no, it
was too far to come at night. Her eyes seemed to fill up.
I explained it wasn't that I didn't want her, it was just
such a long trip. She asked me what she could bring the
next time. I asked for something to read.

When she came back she brought *Life* and *Time* and
Newsweek and *Look* and the *Saturday Evening Post* and
the *Reader's Digest,* all the magazines I had always
wanted to read every week, the magazines I felt I should
keep up with but could never afford. She brought me two
cartons of cigarettes. I had never had two cartons at
a time. She slipped everything into the drawer, and we
tried to hold a conversation for a little while, and then
I told her to go before it got too late. After she left,
I reached into the drawer for a cigarette. There were
two rolls of dimes in there for the telephone, and some
cigarette money. One hundred dollars. I counted it five
times. I couldn't believe it because it was just like
Momma would have acted if she were a rich girl like
Lillian Smith. When I got out on a three-day pass from
the hospital, I took Lillian to a movie. She was so happy,
it was like offering her the world.

I went right back to work after I got out of the hospital, and it was like romping and stomping through
the neighborhood after the levee and the prom and the
Wood River meet and the senior class speech all wrapped
into one Friday night where the customers stood and
clapped and cheered when I walked back up on my stage.
Only they weren't clapping for any gladiator, they were
saying, Man, we're really glad you're back, we missed
you, like how was it? Did a hell of a show that night,
just talking about the hospital, the nurses, the doctors, the
other patients, and when it was over everybody crowded
around and told me they were planning to come out and
visit me next week, or they would have sent me a card but
they didn't have the address, and they said it like they
meant it. Somebody brought me some flowers. Oh, man,
I kept romping and stomping all that fall, and my shows
got better and better, and the lines got longer and longer,

and more and more people were coming out just to hear me. Lil and I were going out pretty often now, and I'd carry her out to the club to see my act, and we'd talk about my work and she'd type up material for me at her job. I was such a big man now I went right up to the Esquire owners and I told them I was due for a raise. Been here almost a year, I'm packing the place every night, and ten dollars a night just isn't enough money for a comic like me. I want twelve dollars a night. They told me ten dollars a night was plenty. I told them if they didn't give me a two dollar raise I'd quit on them. They didn't give me a raise.

When I quit the Esquire I had the same funny feeling in my stomach I had when I left college with nowhere to go. Everything, everyone was behind me. I spent most of December lying around the house, reading and watching television. Toward Christmas I played a couple benefits, just to make me feel I was still an entertainer. It was at one of those benefit shows that somebody mentioned there was an old, vacant night club for rent out in Robbins, Illinois. It was owned by a woman named Sally Wells. I called her, and she said the rent was fifty-six dollars a night. I told her not to make a move until we could get together.

Ira Murchison drove me out in his car the next day, a nineteen-mile trip, and I talked nonstop the whole way. My own night club. I could do anything I wanted. I'd be my own boss. I'd do more topical material and less blue material. I'd gain respect as an owner and a performer. I'd develop new talent. I'd pay good salaries. I'd create an atmosphere for good comedy. Everybody would be happy. Ira didn't say a word. He didn't even ask me what I was going to use for money.

Sally Wells was a woman in her seventies, and the Apex Club was the most raggedy-looking night club in the world, a small, dusty, creaky, empty room. It looked a little haunted. We were peeking around the room, the three of us, when Sally Wells suddenly turned to Ira and stared at him with her bright, glittering eyes.

"You've been overseas," she said, mysteriously, "and you're going back again."

"Yeah, that's right, how you know?" said Ira. The year before, he had represented the United States in the Moscow track meet, and was planning to go again.

Then she turned on me, and I had the same strange feeling I had twenty years before when one of Momma's spiritualist readers said she saw a star in the middle of my head.

"I see you flying all over this country, from one end to another, with a little brown case in your hand," said Sally Wells.

Now I was really impressed. I had always had the idea, for some reason, that all the top comics carried their material in brown leather briefcases.

"I also see you getting married soon."

"Nope, you're wrong there. There's a little matter of having to be in love first."

Sally Wells shook her head. "I see you getting married."

I humored her because I was trying to make a business deal, and then we changed the subject. We sat and we talked and figured things out. I'd pay her $168 a week, for using the club Fridays, Saturdays, and Sundays. There was insurance and licenses and cleaning and heat and electricity and water and taxes. By the time Ira and I left Robbins and headed back north to Chicago, Dick Gregory was in business.

One of the first things I did was borrow $800 from Lillian, my rich ace in the hole. We had gotten pretty close. Then I went to every newspaper in Chicago, white and Negro, and took out ads. In the big papers, good-sized ads with printed directions for getting out to Robbins cost sixty-five dollars a day. I was going first-class. I bought glasses and tables and chairs. Went around to entertainers I knew, and hired a band and some acts. I knew I'd need a car, and Maryann had one. I asked her if she would like to be my head cashier. She was fascinated by the idea. I hired a few other girls I knew as waitresses. Then I went to buy whiskey. I had never been much of a drinker, but I learned more about liquor in two weeks than most people learn in a lifetime. Scotch, bourbon, gin, vodka, rye, wines, brandies, and every kind has a dozen different brands. I finally talked a liquor-store owner on Sixty-third and St. Lawrence into letting me have $1,000 worth of liquor for the first weekend. I would pay for only what was used and opened, bring everything else back. I convinced him that when I hit it big with the club he'd get all my business. Then all I needed was beer, and different kinds of soda.

That first Friday in January I loaded everything into the car and headed out to Robbins. Opening night was only hours away. Halfway out, I realized I had no change. I drove back to town and persuaded Ozelle, my land-lady, to borrow change from her boss at the drugstore. She had to promise to stand good for $100 worth of silver. Halfway out again, I remembered I'd need ice for the beer and cubes for the drinks. Back again, out again. Then lemons. Then pick up two of the waitresses, one singer, and the girl who owned the car.

At seven o'clock I opened the doors of the Apex Club and leaned back with a smirky smile to watch the people trample each other in the mad dash to get in. By nine o'clock there were four customers. They got very good service. At ten we had a dozen, mostly friends, but by eleven o'clock the Apex Club was more than half filled and, baby, I'm a night-club owner. I never worked so hard in my life.

Did I ever move that night! One of the acts hasn't shown up, run out and call them . . . introduce the band . . . a guy comes in without a tie, hustle him out . . . run out of change, scuffle up some more . . . introduce the singer . . . need more lemons . . . guy without a tie is back, hustle him out again . . . introduce the dancer . . . customer isn't satisfied, go pacify him . . . money drawer is stuck, unstick it . . . somebody wants a fancy drink, go buy a bottle of crème de menthe . . . introduce the guitar player . . . glasses are coming out of the kitchen dirty,

send them back and bawl out the waitresses . . . guy
without a tie is back, go get him one . . . two men get up
to fight, jump in between them . . . more change . . .
customer says he was short-changed, a lie, but give him
money anyway . . . go up and do my act, a masterpiece
of a show . . . another fight, calm them down and buy
them drinks . . . drawer stuck . . . more change . . . more
lemons . . . more change . . . more change . . . time to
close, clear everybody out . . . count the liquor . . . count
the money . . . put the beer back in the cases . . . Cokes
back in the cartons . . . load everything in the car because one robbery here will wipe me out . . . drive back
to Chicago . . . too tired to carry everything inside . . .
sleep in the car.

Saturday night we had a big, live crowd, a full house.
It was twice as wild as Friday night, and I worked ten
times as hard, and it was beautiful. I got up onstage and
I gave two great shows, mostly topical material right out
of the newspapers. And by the time we closed up we
had $1,200 in the till. I couldn't believe it. I didn't know
whether I was opening a club or closing it, I was so tired,
but I knew I had $1,200 in a sack. We ran afternoon
and evening shows that Sunday to fairly respectable
houses.

By Monday morning I was in the pawnshop and at
friends' houses, scraping up enough to pay the next week's
ads and rent. The $1,200 wasn't mine very long, with
all the back bills. The only performers I paid for the
first weekend were the bandsmen—they belonged to a
union that would have closed the place. But I wasn't
more than $1,000 in debt now, and things were rolling,
and I knew after the second weekend I'd be almost clear,
and after that I'd have to hire someone to help me count
the money. I saved that expense at least. The next Friday
we got thirteen inches of snow. Thirteen inches of snow
and three customers.

I stood in the back of my club that night and I swore
that when I really hit it big and went to appear in another man's night club I would refuse to take a penny

if the weather was so bad that nobody showed up. I would never take a cent if there was a tornado or a hurricane or a blizzard. I thought about that for a while. I had time that night. Yeah, I thought, that's okay when you're thinking as an owner, Greg, but don't forget all those ten-dollar nights at the Esquire when you showed up on bad nights even when the customers didn't. You were going there to make your rent money, not spend it.

Saturday came with five more inches of snow and sleet, too. The highways were bad and we were nineteen miles out of downtown Chicago. Twenty people showed up. There were twenty on Sunday, and two more inches of snow. It was only the beginning of one of the worst winters we ever had in Chicago. The third and fourth weekends had snow and sleet and hail and freezing rain. Most nights there were more employees than customers in the Apex Club. I paid the girls with promises, promises that the weather would break, that we'd hit it big, that they'd all get their back pay and more. They believed me. I borrowed more money to keep the place going. I pawned and sold everything I could get my hands on. I began to resent the bandsmen who didn't drink heavily on the job. They weren't leaving their salaries in the club. The liquor-store owner began to complain because I was bringing too much whiskey back, so I began to start each night with a pint each of gin, vodka, bourbon, and Scotch, six cans of beer, and a couple of cartons of soda. As I sold out, I'd run out to a small package store across the street and buy more. There were nights I didn't have to buy more. And the rent went on, and the advertising went on. I was sinking so far into debt I couldn't see straight.

On Thursday, January 29, 1959, I decided it was time to play my ace in the hole again. My rich girl. I went to see Lillian Smith. She was very sweet, but apologetic. All she could give me was $300. She had quit her job at the University and she was leaving town. I had to ask her twice before she told me why.

"I'm pregnant, Greg. I'm going to have a baby."

The words felt as though someone had taken a bucket

of ice water and splashed it against my naked guts. That's all I need now, a baby, everything I'm trying for, everything I'm killing myself for, and no money, and no real home, and I don't want to bring up any baby that's going to be brought up as poor as I was brought up.

We sat and we talked and I asked Lil questions. No, she wasn't rich—she had saved some money for college and when she left after a year she had kept the money in the bank. She had already given most of it to me. Yes she had known about this for some time, she was about four months pregnant. But you've been so busy and working so hard, Greg, I just didn't want to . . . and now I'm not listening to her and I'm thinking that as poor as the Gregory kids were, and as ornery and as rotten and as no-good as Big Pres was, at least we all had a name. Big Pres had given us that.

I asked Lil to marry me.

She refused. She said she didn't want to do anything to stand in my way.

This time I didn't ask her, I told her. Friday we got the blood tests and bought the license, and on Monday, February 2, 1959, I was a married man. Old lady Wells was right.

At midnight on Monday, Lil and I got on a Greyhound Bus for St. Louis. Three hundred miles down, sleeting all the way through the night. I told her that everything would be all right, the weather would break soon, the night club would hit, and I'd bring her back to Chicago and be a husband and a father. She was very brave. Lil was going to a city where she knew no one, to live with people she barely knew existed. I had no idea how hard it was going to be for her, then.

That Tuesday was one of the worst days St. Louis ever had. Rain and snow and driving sleet. The buses weren't running, there were no cabs, and the insurance companies had announced that no cars would be covered that day. We finally found a guy bootlegging rides and he took us to the project where my sister Dolores lived with her three kids. Dolores was separated from her husband and was working as a waitress. Times were tough for her, too. But she was good and kind and she welcomed Lil. I saw some of my kinfolk in St. Louis and I asked everybody to help, and I talked to Lil some more. Then I went back to Chicago and the Apex Club.

III

It's impossible to be in the night-club business for six months and never make a penny. Absolutely impossible. I'll never believe it happened to me.

Somehow it seemed as though the harder we worked, the worse the weather got. There were weeks in February and March when the weather would break clear and warmer on Wednesday and I'd tell the waitresses who had never been paid, and the friends who had gone to a finance company for me, and the head cashier who had taken a second job to give me liquor money—I was right, baby, here we go now, this is the weekend this beautiful thing happens. Then Friday would smash down on us with snow and sleet and 10 degrees. There were nights I was so tired and confused and half crazy that I thought the winter was a giant trick created just for me, a way for God to test my soul.

I'd go up on stage and be funny and develop and try not to think of what I was going to say to the bill collector at the side table when I came down again. By March I couldn't afford to advertise any more, or pay my room rent to Ozelle and William, or the club rent to Sally Wells. The Underwoods themselves were sinking deeper into debt over me, and Sally Wells was laying out money for my heat, electricity, water, license, and taxes. The night-club acts haven't been paid in so long that they're hassling with me and with each other. The husband and wife team is splitting up, and the girl singer is fighting every night with her boy friend, and the only thing I can give these people is hope and free liquor. But the hope is wearing thin, and my friends are pawning their clothes to pay my whiskey bill. And behind everything else is the realization that I have to hit by May because

I don't want my baby born in a city hospital. There were nights when I ran across the street for another half-pint that all I wanted to do was pass the liquor store and turn the corner and put my head down and lift my knees and salute the lamppost and take off, just keep running, Greg, just keep running.

I never sent Lil a penny, and by April I couldn't afford to call St. Louis any more. Then the Underwoods' telephone was turned off for nonpayment.

Some of my friends began to turn against me. I couldn't blame them. You can't keep saying "Tomorrow" to a man who borrowed $500 for you and now his paycheck is being garnisheed and he might lose his job. You can't say "Tomorrow" to Thelma Isbell, a woman with three children who might be put out of her apartment, to people who are going to lose things they pawned for you. But you say tomorrow and you say next week, and then tomorrow and next week roll around and you have to explain it to them all over again. The snow is going to melt and the sun is going to come out and the Apex Club is going to have a real, live crowd again, maybe tomorrow, maybe next week. You say it when Ozelle is sick, and William is laid off, and the waitresses' children are hungry. You say it when you're lying on the floor, too weary to put up your hands just enough to keep your friend from punching you in the face again. Just lie there and wish you were dead and know you couldn't be that lucky. And know that as bad as things are, they are ten times worse for Lillian, living with strangers in a strange city, waiting for a baby whose father never calls.

The second week in May, a man walked into the Apex Club with a gun. There were six customers in the club that night, and they jumped up and ran out. The waitresses and the bandsmen and the acts flattened out against the walls and froze when he walked around the tables, kicking chairs out of his way and waving the gun at the girl behind the money drawer. I came down off the stage and walked right up to him and looked him right in the eyes.

"Look, mister, you don't know what I've been through,

or you wouldn't come in here with that gun, you'd come in here with money."

He looked at me as if I were crazy, and he motioned me out of his way with the gun. I didn't move. I was crazy. "Listen, mister, one of us has to die tonight. What I've gone through all winter with this place, you need to pull a gun and shoot me to run me out of here. God Himself couldn't run me out of here, and He's tried."

The man looked at me and shook his head. He had been down to the nitty-gritty himself, I guess, because he put his gun back in his pocket and said he was sorry. He turned and walked out.

I scuffled up enough money that week to have the Underwoods' phone turned back on, and the first call that came through was Dolores, and she said the baby was due in another week. She had taken Lil to the City Hospital for an examination. I put down the phone and I sat next to it for a long time, as if there were someone I could call to say: "Give me another month or so on this, just a little more time and the weather'll break and the crowds'll come out to Robbins, and I'll be able to take care of this thing right."

I went to a friend of mine that day, Pat Toomey, a man I had been avoiding. "I know I owe you some money," I said, "but a man has two ways of borrowing. He can ask and he can tell. I'm telling you. I need bus fare to St. Louis. One way. My baby'll be born next week."

"I didn't know you were married, Greg."

"No one knows."

Pat gave me the money and I went right down to St. Louis. The first thing I did when I got off the bus was walk three miles to the Red Cross office. I gave them my name at the desk, and took a seat. While I was waiting to be called, I looked over the Red Cross workers at their desks and picked out a nice-looking, gray-haired lady. She had a warm, friendly face. She would understand. I'd make a deal: if the Red Cross lent me money so my baby could be born in a private hospital, I would give them half of everything I'd ever make in my life. The weather is going to clear and then I'm going to hit it big, starting next week, and you can't afford to turn this deal down.

"Mister Gregory?" It was a man, in the far corner.

I sat down and I explained the situation. I told him I had a night club in Chicago, that I was an entertainer temporarily broke, and that the baby was due the next week.

"You know, Mister Gregory, we have a very fine city hospital right here in St. Louis, and your wife will be well taken care of. Let me give you the address."

I didn't tell him that I knew the address, that I could remember the day a doctor slapped me and cursed my Momma in that very fine city hospital. How could I explain to him, a man I was begging from, that I didn't want my kid born in a city hospital?

"Thank you, sir," I said. "Thank you very much for your time. I guess you're right."

I walked out of the Red Cross office, and around the block and down the street, walking and praying and thinking and suddenly I had an idea. I started running. When Ron was at Notre Dame he got a hernia, and a doctor from St. Louis operated on him for free. I ran to a phone booth and started looking through the book until the name came to me. He had an office across town. I ran right over. And paced in front of it for two hours until I had the courage to walk into the office of a white doctor who didn't even know me. He was sitting there with a pleasant smile.

"I'm Dick Gregory, Ron Gregory's brother, and . . ."

"Why, of course, I remember Ron, you know that day he took the mile at the . . ."

We sat there and we talked, and I talked about Notre Dame as if I had built that school with my own two hands, and I talked about Ron as if I had lived in his soul. Whenever we were ready to stop talking I'd talk some more, just to put off begging from a white man I didn't even know. He must have sensed it on my face, or forty-five minutes was just as long as a doctor could take.

"By the way, is there anything I can do to help you?"

"Yes, sir. I have a wife here in St. Louis that's going to have a baby next week. I have no money."

He reached into his pocket and pulled out his wallet. "How much do you need?"

The world stood still and turned beautiful, and I remembered when I was a kid and had a wallet, and an angel came down and whispered something, and I was so happy and bursting inside I could never have believed man had ever fought a war or hated or been cruel.

"I said how much will you need, Mister Gregory?"

"I don't know, Doctor. How much does it cost to have a baby?"

He called his nurse in. "Would you call the hospital and make an appointment for . . . what's your wife's name?"

"Lillian Gregory."

". . . for Lillian Gregory. Tell them she'll be in next week, and that they should hold the bill for me."

"Doctor, I don't know how to thank you, I . . ."

The blood was running through my veins again, and I wanted to kiss him and hug him and give him all the joys and pleasures I ever had in my whole life. When I got out on the street again I talked to the trees and the birds and I nodded at the police car and I ran all the way to my sister's house and I couldn't wait for the elevator so I ran up eleven flights of stairs and burst into the apartment and grabbed a wife I hardly knew and hadn't seen in almost four months. "Hey, baby, let me tell you what happened today."

She sat there, her face shining. "Oh, Greg, oh, Greg," and I was talking fast again. I told her what to do and where to go and how she was going to be all right. Now, baby, I've got to find some money to get back to Chicago and open up the Apex Club tomorrow night. Somehow she understood, even though she shouldn't have had to.

I went by my aunt's house, and they started screaming at me, what a disgrace you are, doing a woman like you're doing. I tried to explain to them this thing I had, that it was bigger than you and me and my wife and the baby. They started screaming again, and I had to leave my aunt's house running. I got some bus fare for myself and some carfare for Lil, and I went back to Dolores'. My sister was home and she took me aside. Lil wasn't eating, she wasn't talking or doing much of anything. She sat around the house taking care of Dolores' kids and sleeping and crying, sleeping and crying. Lil was crying when I left the apartment, and as I slammed the door behind me I heard her scream, "Please don't leave me again." I went back into the apartment and into the room where she was sobbing on the bed, and she looked up and said: "I'm sorry, Greg, please forgive me." All the way back to Chicago I tried to figure out how a woman could understand what a man was trying to do the way Lil understood. And she didn't even know me yet.

It was another miserable weekend in Chicago, raining from Friday to Sunday. This time, it didn't matter too much. I had met a man who reached for his wallet, and my kid wasn't going to be born in a city hospital. On Wednesday night, Dolores called and told me everything was fine. Lil had been thoroughly examined and had been admitted to the hospital that afternoon. The baby was due at any time. Everything was working according to plan. I felt great. My stomach quieted down.

The phone rang again on Thursday evening.

"Richard?"

"Yeah, is . . ."

"Richard, to the last day you live you'll never be forgiven what happened to this woman, you'll . . ."

"What are you talking about?"

"Your baby's born, Richard."

"Is that right? Wonderful! How's Lil?"

"She's here in the house, Richard, and the baby's here in the house, and both of them laying there on the floor . . ."

"But Lil's at the hospital, she's . . ."

"They sent her home, again, Richard. They said . . ."

"You call the ambulance?"

"Yeah, they on their way, Richard, you . . ."

"Let me talk to her, Dolores . . . Dolores?"

"Richard, she just lying in there, lying on her back on

the floor, lookin' up at her baby. The hospital told me to put the baby on top of her stomach . . ."

"Dolores, oh, God, Dolores, is she really there on the floor?"

"Yeah, Richard."

"But I thought she was in the hospital."

"She was there all night, Richard, all night long. They acted kind of funny to her, and she's such a strange woman, that Lil. She wasn't having labor pains so they told her she could go home, and she came home and then she had the pains and she was all alone in the house and she didn't have no cab fare, honest to God, Richard, she didn't have no cab fare, and she just . . ."

"Dolores?"

"I can't hear you, Richard."

"Dolores, did she holler much?"

"She hasn't said nothing. I've had three babies, Richard, and I always hollered, but she didn't say a word. I came home, Richard, and if I didn't go into the room I wouldn't know she was in there having her baby on the floor . . ."

"I can't believe it, Dolores, oh, my God . . ."

"The ambulance's here, Richard . . ."

I hung up the phone, and the next thing I knew I was running through the rain, just running like a crazy man, and I ran around a corner and right into a guy I knew from the University track team, Brooks Johnson. We both fell down on the sidewalk. Before we got up, I said: "Would you loan me ten dollars?" He never asked why, just reached in his pocket, and then I was up running again, from the South Side down to the Loop, and I caught the St. Louis bus just as it was pulling out. I fell asleep the moment I sat down, and slept for seven hours, all the way to St. Louis. Then I ran to Dolores' house.

"Richard, oh, Richard, the elevator was so small they had to stand her up on the stretcher going down eleven floors with the baby against her stomach . . ."

"Where is she, Dolores?"

"Homer G. Phillips."

The City Hospital. The old place haunted me down after all. I went right over there, marched up to the desk, and told them I wanted to see my wife. Where is she?

"What is her name, sir?"

"Mrs. Richard Gregory."

"Certainly, sir. She's on the fourth floor. Let me give you a slip of paper so you can visit your daughter."

Lil was in a ward with twenty other women. Some of them were tossing and groaning, and I was scared to go in. I finally did, and Lil looked up at me, and all she said was: "Hi, Greg, I'm sorry."

"Oh, Lil, don't be sorry for nothing. It was . . . oh, God, Lil, are you all right?"

She smiled. "I'm just fine, Greg." She waved her hand to make me come closer, and she whispered: "Greg, would you mind saying something nice to the lady in the bed over there? I've been telling her all about you."

I did, and then I went up to see my baby girl, and then I spent some more time with Lil, and then I looked at my baby again, and then I went back down to the fourth floor.

"It's Friday, Lil, I got to go back and open up the club."

"I understand, Greg. We'll be all right, don't you worry."

When the bandsmen walked into the Apex Club that night, I was standing by the door and I told every one of them that I was a Daddy and if they wanted to hold onto their jobs they better bring gifts for my baby. I walked around that weekend in a daze, sometimes proud because I was a father, sometimes ashamed because of what Lil had gone through all alone. On Tuesday I went back down to St. Louis with a hundred dollars worth of baby gifts and fifty dollars I scuffled up for Lil. It was the first time I ever brought anything to my wife. It felt like fifty million dollars to a guy who had let his wife pay for the ring and the blood test and the license and the bus fare out of town more than four months ago. For the first time I began to feel like a husband and a father.

Lil was home from the hospital, and I spent three days with her, the first time we ever spent any time together as husband and wife. It was the first time I lay in bed with my wife, and touched my wife, and put my back next to my wife's back, and closed my eyes and slept next to my wife. And she was so beautiful, she just lay there and told me how happy she was, and I couldn't believe it.

I never will forget how I lay there and tried to tell her that I knew what she had been through, that I knew she had to hate me, that I didn't blame her. She cried and shook her head and said: "Hate you for what, Greg? You're going to be the biggest entertainer in show business some day, and you did what you had to do. Some day you'll sit back and you'll see we didn't go through anything."

I couldn't believe this woman existed. We slept and we talked and we cried and laughed together for three days, and we began to know each other. So shy and bashful, that little girl I married, and now she was a woman. We talked about naming the baby. Michele Rene Gregory.

"You know, Greg, when I was lying on that floor I thought—Dick Gregory's child is going to say: 'Dick Gregory's my Daddy,' never going to say: 'I was born on the floor.' Just say: 'Dick Gregory's my Daddy.' You can do anything you want to do, Greg—you know that and I know that—and don't let anything stop you."

I told Lil that I was thinking about quitting show business. Hell, I'm nothing but a peon, never worked in a big night club, never even been inside of one. She shook her head and touched my cheek. We held each other very tight those days and nights in St. Louis, and I began to discover who I had married, and I found out I loved her, and I learned, again, how a woman can give strength.

"Those things you told me about your mother, Greg," Lil would say, "if she could do all those things for six of you, I can do anything you want me to do. I understand you can't always come down here. I look for you every day, and when the day is gone and the week is gone, I just keep seeing you coming. And I know you're on your way."

I went back to Chicago that weekend, and the weather was clear and bright and warm, and the highways were dry and smooth and the Apex Club was packed. It was June and the long winter was over. Real live crowds now. The money was starting to come in. We're going to hit, baby, because we suffered through the whole storm, and now the weather has broken. June went, and July came, and there were lines outside the door. Every time I stood on that stage I felt the monster seep right up me, and I was funny and every show was a masterpiece. I had spent six months in my own night club creating and developing my own comedy. The crowds came and the Apex Club was beginning to really hit.

I lost the night club in July.

Old lady Wells was very nice, but there was all that money I owed her, and she was getting on in years. There were some buyers looking over the place now. The place had a name. This was the time to sell. Sally Wells gave me a chance. There was the money I owed her for the licenses and the heat and the electricity and the water and the taxes. There was four months worth of back rent: fifty-six dollars a night times three nights a week four weeks to a month times four months.

"Has to be in by Sunday, Mister Gregory."

That was it. There were no more tomorrows or next weeks, there were no more people to borrow money from. The last weekend the owners-to-be came out and looked the place over again, and smiled at each other at the size of the crowd. I remember giving my show while they walked around the room and talked to each other about how they would decorate the club when they took it over.

Well, we went out like champs. After the last show on Sunday night we threw a big party, and drank and danced and talked. But mostly cried. We had worked together through one of the worst winters in Chicago and we hadn't made any money, but for six months, every Friday, Saturday, and Sunday, we could look forward to being somebodies, to being part of something ethical and honest and decent, a place where the customer was always treated right and the employees got respect, a night club that had never had gambling or prostitution or bootleg whiskey, a night club that—for us—had been something like a home.

It was early in the morning before that party broke up. I looked at those sad faces, and I made a speech. I thanked them for their faith. I told them what they had seen. A boy had turned into a man before their eyes. I told them, if you carry fifty pounds on your back and don't weaken, you strengthen your back to carry a hundred, and then a thousand, and if that doesn't break you, some day you'll be able to carry the world. And walk with it. That's how strong I feel.

At dawn, I walked down the steps of the Apex Club for the last time, thinking of all the trails I had made across the street, the people I had known, the lessons I had learned, the tests I had passed. Good-by, Apex good-by and thank you so much. There will be no turning back now.

I'm ready.

IV

I lost the Apex Club in the summer of 1959, and the next year and a half was up and down, in and out, hustling and scuffling and pestering people to listen to me, hire me, pay me. But I was moving now, and tasting that thing. The Apex had put the monster back in me for good. In August I got my old job back at the Esquire, at ten dollars a night. I started bugging Herman Roberts, the owner of the biggest Negro night club in America, to come out and catch my act. He wouldn't move. So I brought the mountain to him. The Pan-American Games were in Chicago that year, and I knew a lot of the athletes. I borrowed some money, and rented Roberts Show Club for one night to throw a party for the teams. Naturally, it was a one-man show. Afterwards, Herman Roberts came up to me and asked how much I wanted to be master of ceremonies at his club. I said $125 a week. He nearly slipped and said: "Is that all?"

All the top Negro acts played Roberts in those days—Sarah Vaughan, Count Basie, Sammy Davis, Jr., Billy Eckstine, Nipsey Russell, Dinah Washington. There was Red Saunders' big house band, an eight-girl chorus line, and more than a thousand seats. When I stood on that electrically powered stage and introduced the acts and gave the coming attractions, I felt like a top Negro act, too. I rented a furnished apartment for $25 a week and brought Lil and Michele into Chicago. The kitchen was in the basement, but it was home and we were together. Told everybody I was on my way. Had me a few words with that dumb Esquire management. Too quick. The Roberts job folded a month later; I didn't know he only kept his M.C.'s four weeks at a time.

Lil got her old job back at the University of Chicago, and we bought a ten-year-old Plymouth for fifty dollars. No insurance and no floorboards, but every day, with six-month-old Michele on the front seat, the old car made the rounds. Booking agents, night-club owners, people who knew people. Now and then we'd come up with something, ten dollars here, fifty there, once a $175-a-week gig at a white honky-tonk. I lasted only a week there. Told the management they'd have to stop those B-girls from tricking the tourists so badly if they wanted to retain an artist of my caliber.

So Michele grew a little older in the front seat of that Plymouth. She never cried, never carried on, just lay there all wrapped up in blankets against the wind coming in from underneath. We pestered more people, kept going around to the union, the American Guild of Variety Artists. On Monday nights, AGVA members got a chance to audition in front of an audience of white night-club owners and agents. Every time I asked them to put me on an AGVA night they asked me if I could sing or dance.

"I'm a comedian, sir."

"We'll have an opening for you in about a year and a half."

Whenever things got too tight, I'd pick up a little money washing cars, doing little things here and there. Then Herman Roberts called again. Only ten dollars a night to start during this time, and I'd have to help the waiters seat the customers during the Sammy Davis, Jr., engagement. But I could stay for as long as I was funny. It was at Roberts that I learned one of the greatest lessons in show business.

Sammy Davis, Jr., and Nipsey Russell were appearing on the same bill at Roberts, probably the biggest attraction the club ever had. They were playing to 90-per-cent white audiences, and for many of those customers it was their first trip to the South Side of Chicago. For most, it was the first time they had ever been to the South Side at night. The Club was packed with white executives who were slipping the waiters fifty-dollar tips for ringside tables. Nipsey would open the show, with a lot of racial comedy, and he absolutely slayed that white audience. They couldn't laugh hard enough. Nipsey stole that show, even against Sammy Davis with all his talents. I couldn't believe it. I tried to figure it out.

A few nights after Nipsey had opened at Roberts, he was called down for an AGVA night. The word had gotten out how well he was going over uptown. I went downtown that Monday night to a white club and watched Nipsey work that audience of white night-club owners. It was the same routine he had killed the customers with at Roberts, but that night Nipsey just sat up there and died. He couldn't get the same response he got at Roberts.

And then I began to figure it out. A white man will come to the Negro club, so hung up in this race problem, so nervous and afraid of the neighborhood and the people that anything the comic says to relieve his tension will absolutely knock him out. The harder that white man laughs, the harder he's saying, "I'm all right, boy, it's that Other Man downtown." That white customer in the Negro club is filled with guilt and filled with fear. I've seen a white man in a Negro club jump up and say "Excuse me" to a Negro waitress who just spilled a drink in his lap. If that same thing happened in a white night club, that man would jump up, curse, and call his lawyer. That was the kind of audience that Nipsey slayed in the Roberts Show Club. But when Nipsey went downtown for AGVA night he was in the white man's house, and the white man felt comfortable and secure. He didn't have to laugh at racial material that he really didn't want to hear.

This gave me something to think about, to work with. Some day I'm going to be performing where the bread is, in the big white night clubs. When I step up on that stage, in *their* neighborhood, some of them are going to feel sorry for me because I'm a Negro, and some of them are going to hate me because I'm a Negro. Those who feel sorry might laugh a little at first. But they can't respect someone they pity, and eventually they'll stop laughing. Those who hate me aren't going to laugh at all.

I've got to hit them fast, before they can think, just the way I hit those kids back in St. Louis who picked on me because I was raggedy and had no Daddy. I've got to go up there as an individual first, a Negro second. I've got to be a colored funny man, not a funny colored man. I've got to act like a star who isn't sorry for himself— that way, they can't feel sorry for me. I've got to make jokes about myself, before I can make jokes about them and their society—that way, they can't hate me. Comedy is friendly relations.

"Just my luck, bought a suit with two pair of pants today . . . burnt a hole in the jacket."

That's making fun of yourself.

"They asked me to buy a lifetime membership in the NAACP, but I told them I'd pay a week at a time. Hell of a thing to buy a lifetime membership, wake up one morning and find the country's been integrated."

That makes fun of the whole situation.

Now they're listening to you, and you can blow a cloud of smoke at the audience and say:

"Wouldn't it be a hell of a thing if all this was burnt cork and you people were being tolerant for nothing?"

Now you've got them. No bitterness, no Uncle Tomming. We're all aware of what's going on here, aren't we, baby? Now you can settle down and talk about anything you want: Fall-out shelters, taxes, mothers-in-law, sit-ins, freedom riders, the Congo, H-bomb, the President, children. Stay away from sex, that's the big pitfall. If you use blue material only, you slip back into being that Negro stereotype comic. If you mix blue and topical satire that white customer, all hung up with the Negro sex mystique, is going to get uncomfortable.

In and out of Roberts in 1960, I had plenty of time to think. I realized that when I started working the white clubs, one of my big problems was going to be hecklers —especially in the beginning when I'd be in honky-tonk white clubs. Handling a heckler just right is very important to a comic. Unless you're well known as an insulting comedian you can't chop hecklers down too hard or the crowd will turn against you. Most hecklers are half drunk anyway, and you will lose a crowd if you get mean with a drunk. On the other hand, you have to put a heckler down. If a heckler gets the best of you, that crowd will start to feel sorry for you. I had worked it out pretty well in the Negro clubs. I'd put a drunken heckler down gently: "Man, I'd rather be your slave than your liver," and that would go even better in a white club. Whenever I got a vicious heckler, I could say something like: "Now how would you like it if I came to *your* job and kicked the shovel out of *your* hand?" That would work fine, too. But some day, somewhere, I'd be in a white club and somebody would get up and call me a nigger.

I worried about that. When that white man calls me nigger, every other white man in that club is going to feel embarrassed. The customers are going to tie in that uncomfortable feeling with that club—even after I'm gone— and the club owner knows this. He would rather keep me out of his club than take a chance on losing customers. It was the same thing when I got kicked in the mouth as a shoeshine boy—the bartender ran me out of the place, even though he felt sorry for me, because he couldn't afford to have the customers fight. But now I'm a man and I have to take care of myself. I need a fast comeback to that word. That split second is all the difference between going on with the show or letting the customers feel pity and a little resentment for the enter-tainer who got put down.

I used to make Lillian call me a nigger over the din-ner table, and I'd practice the fast comeback. Somehow,

I couldn't get it right. I'd always come back with something a little bitter, a little evil.

"Nigger."

"Maybe you'd feel more like a man if you lived down South and had a toilet with your name on it."

"No, Greg, that's not right at all."

I was lying around the house one night, watching television and feeling mad at the world. I'd been out of work for three weeks. The snow was so deep I hadn't even been outside the house for four days. Lil was sitting in a corner, so calm and peaceful, reading a book. There was no one else to pick on.

"Hey, Lil."

"Yes, Greg."

"What would you do if from here on in I started referring to you as bitch?"

She jumped out of the chair. "I would simply ignore you."

I fell off the couch and started laughing so hard that old stomach of mine nearly burst. That was it. The quick, sophisticated answer. Cool. No bitterness. The audience would never know I was mad and mean inside. And there would be no time to feel sorry for me. Now I'd get that comeback.

I got my chance a few weeks later, in a run-down neighborhood club on the outskirts of town. The customers were working-class white men, laborers, factory hands, men whose only marks of dignity were the Negroes they bossed on the job and kept away from on weekends. It happened in the middle of the late show on the second night. Loud and clear.

"Nigger."

The audience froze, and I wheeled around without batting an eye. "You hear what that guy just called me? Roy Rogers' horse. He called me Trigger."

I had hit them so quick that they laughed, and they laughed hard because that was what they really wanted to believe the guy had called me. But I had only bought myself a little time. There was an element in the house that really knew what he had called me. I had the crowd locked up with that fast comeback, so I took a few seconds to look them over and blow out some smoke.

"You know, my contract reads that every time I hear that word, I get fifty dollars more a night. I'm only making ten dollars a night, and I'd like to put the owner out of business. Will everybody in the room please stand up and yell nigger?"

They laughed and they clapped and I swung right back into my show. Afterwards, the owner came over and gave me twenty dollars and shook my hand and thanked me. I had made my test.

The weather broke, and Michele and I got back into the Plymouth and made our rounds. Another gig in a white club, a little place in Mishawaka, Indiana, ninety-eight miles from Chicago on the other side of South Bend. I drove the distance every night because at ten dollars I couldn't afford a hotel. That club was a big thing in Mishawaka, and the white folks lined up early to get in. It was on a Saturday night, the place was packed, and I kept noticing a group of white girls sitting on the lounge chairs near the back. They were drinking pretty heavily, and laughing at all the wrong places.

Suddenly, one of the girls shouted: "You're handsome."

Every white man in the place froze. That's that sex angle, thrown right in your face, and the whole room hates you for it. Okay, here we go.

"Honey, what nationality are you?"

"Hungarian."

"Take another drink. You'll think you're Negro. Then you'll run up here and kiss me and we'll both have to leave town in a hurry."

That busted it. The room came all the way down again, and you could hear the relief in that explosion of laughter. If there was any hate left in that room, it was for that girl.

I felt stronger and stronger now, more confident that I could handle anything that came up. I went back into Roberts that summer for another engagement. The Republican Party Convention was in town then, and some

of the delegates went slumming one night and caught my
act. They talked about it. A few nights later, John
Daly's crew from the American Broadcasting Company
came by. He was doing a television documentary about
the race situation in the North, "Cast the First Stone."
He wanted to tape my routine. I was signed to a contract,
got a dollar to make it legal, and a crew came out and
taped me for two hours. I ran all the way home to tell
Lil. This is it. Prime time, baby, network. John Daly.
We have to plan strategy now, make sure everybody in
the whole country sees me on television.

"Lil, you know that paper you type things on at the
University . . ."

"Yeah, Greg . . ."

"Can you get some of it?"

"Sure."

"Now, we'll need about eighty thousand sheets of
that . . ."

Next morning I dressed Michele and drove out to the
University. The lady out there knew Lil and was very
nice, but a little confused. Eighty thousand sheets? Finally we decided to cut a stencil and have someone run it
off on the mimeograph. As soon as I borrowed some
money I'd buy my own paper and pay for the labor.

I had no idea how much 80,000 of anything was until
I picked up those boxes of paper. It was like working the
levee just to load it into the car. Now I have to hand
them out.

It was a simple handbill, it said something like—Make
sure you watch "Cast the First Stone" on September 27,
1960, on the American Broadcasting Company station.
Then write a letter to the network telling them how much
you loved the show, especially Dick Gregory.

For two weeks I passed out those handbills, on street
corners in the Loop, in South Side bars, in restaurants,
outside movie theaters, in schoolyards, outside factories
at lunchtime. Sometimes people read them. Sometimes
people just dropped them on the sidewalk, and I'd run
over and pick them up. It was as if my blood was spilling
on the pavement.

Sometimes it seemed like the more handbills I passed out, the more were left. I borrowed a car with floorboards and drove down to St. Louis and passed them out in front of the high schools, drove down to Carbondale and passed them out in the Student Union. I borrowed some more money for postage stamps and envelopes and started mailing out hundreds at a time to friends and relatives and to every NAACP chapter in the country.

I was still handing them out on street corners the night of the show, mad as hell at all the people who had the nerve to be away from their television sets on a night like this. By the time I got home, the show was fifteen minutes old.

"I been on yet, Lil?"

"Not yet, Greg."

And then it happened. John Daly said something about a new young comic sensation. Right after this message. This is it, baby, hold on. I could see 80,000 letters, at least, in the mail before morning.

8:30. John Daly took about two minutes to introduce me, and there I was, staring at myself on national television, coast-to-coast. Prime time. The whole country was watching me.

Two jokes. Two quick jokes. About twenty seconds. Then it blacked out, and there was a commercial.

"That's a good sign, Lil, a commercial. Means I'll go all the way through the rest of the show. This was just a teaser."

"Sure, Greg."

We sat there until nine o'clock when the program went off, and I never came on again.

"Maybe that was just part one, Greg. Maybe next week they'll have part two."

"Call up and find out."

She did. We stared at each other and cried. Eighty thousand handbills. Twenty seconds. I couldn't believe it. And they had taped my act for more than two hours.

What the hell, back to work. I went into a beatnik coffeehouse off Rush Street, The Fickle Pickle. Seven nights a week, $125 a week, one month. I began to meet

some people who were going to help me. There was Tim
Boxer, a young newspaperman from Canada who was
out of work and sleeping in his car. We got friendly, and
he said he'd do some public relations work for me. There
was Bob Orben, one of the top comedy writers in the
world. I couldn't afford having him write special material
for me, but he sent me his monthly pamphlet of general
jokes, the best school for comics there is today. There
was Joe Musse, who signed me to a contract with Associated Booking, the biggest agents in the country. And
he introduced me to Freddie Williamson in Associated's
Chicago office. Freddie never came to see me work, but
I used to go to his office nearly every day to bug him
into getting me jobs. Between his phone calls and his
other clients, I made Freddie listen to my material. I'd
just stand in his office and do my act for him. He said
he liked it, and that he would try to book me into the
Playboy Club in Chicago. They were always looking for
new talent. Meanwhile, in November of 1960, he got me
a week at Eddie Salem's Supper Club in Akron, Ohio.
I'll never forget that gig.

It was the biggest job I ever had, in the biggest white
club I had ever seen. My first real out-of-town engagement. Two hundred dollars a week and I was on the
same bill with Don Cornell, the singer. A big white club
with a big white star. The response to my material was
pretty good. Eddie Salem let me eat in his club on
credit. He lent me money so I could send Lil enough
for the groceries, and so I could spend money like the
top Negro entertainer I was pretending to be. After my
act I'd sit at the bar like a big man and buy drinks for
the customers. But sooner or later I would have to go
back to my room in the Negro section, a ten-dollar-a-
week room, the only room I could find where I didn't
have to pay a week in advance.

It was on top of a restaurant, and I told the owner
I had just come from a big engagement in Las Vegas
and the only reason I was staying in his place was to
spread a little money around my people. I let racial
prejudice work for me that time.

There was no heat in that room, and one naked light bulb hung from the ceiling. The toilet was broken, and a woman across the hall kept dumping her overnight bucket in the public bathtub. Even when I came back drunk, the stench in that room sobered me up. It was the first time since St. Louis that I had to pile on extra clothes to go to sleep, and when I woke up in the morning, there was a blanket of bugs across the bed. I was cold and miserable and I cried like a baby. I had always stayed away from after-hours joints because I was afraid they would be busted by the police, but I went to every after-hours joint I could find in Akron.

But sooner or later I had to go back to that room, just like sooner or later I used to have to go back to that house on North Taylor. No matter how many track meets I won. It seemed like I was a kid again in high school— all those years and all those things that had happened and I was still coming back to a place with no heat and no light and no running water.

I wasted a lot of tears in Akron. I had no way of knowing I was less than two months away from hitting the big time.

V

Christmas, 1960. Michele had a fever and the apartment was cold and I was out of work again and there were three pounds of fatty white hamburger meat on the table. Poor people are always embarrassed at not having turkey and cranberry sauce for this one day—the same turkey they can't afford in October, the same cranberry sauce they can't afford in May. You try to think that Christmas Day is only twenty-four hours long, just like all the days you were satisfied with beans. But you never really stop believing in Santa Claus. When Momma was Santa Claus you could almost accept having nothing, but when Momma is gone and *you're* Santa Claus you can't accept not being able to give. Maybe that's why honest people steal at Christmas time. Christmas isn't right unless you give.

We didn't really steal that Christmas, but we bought a lot of things we weren't sure we could pay for. First there was the television set. The radio had advertised a set for $114, and Lil and I called up for a demonstration. A man came by the next day with a big television set, plugged it into the wall, and told us that the price was $300. When he found out that the old set we were using belonged to the landlord and that we couldn't trade it in, the price went up to $400. No down payment, seventeen dollars a month for two years. It was a trick, but it was worth it. It was the first piece of furniture Lil and I had ever bought in almost two years of marriage. And it was new, something no one else had ever owned before.

On Christmas Eve, we went down to The Fair, a big department store in the Loop. I sat in the car, nervous, while Lil went inside to try to open a charge account. I was gambling that on Christmas Eve the store was full of stuff they had to get rid of. If Lil said it just right, about her husband being Dick Gregory, the comic, and her being employed by the University of Chicago, they wouldn't question her. After half an hour she came out with her face shining.

"We got it, Greg, up to seventeen hundred dollars."

We bought everything we thought we'd need all year, coats and clothing and blankets and plates and pans and baby things and gifts for kinfolks we had only heard of, and lights for a Christmas tree. We had to hold the packages on our laps so they wouldn't slip through the floor of the car. We only had two dollars in cash, so we bought a raggedy Christmas tree for a dollar, and on the way home we stopped at a grocery and bought three pounds of cheap hamburger meat, thirty-three cents a pound. It was so fatty that the grease overflowed the pan and put the fire out. But Lil ate that hamburger with all the grace in the world, and she fed it to Michele like it was the finest food a mother could offer her daughter. The Gregorys were eating hamburger because it was just what they wanted.

"Honey, this is the last time we'll ever be poor on Christmas, this is the last time you'll ever have to cook a Christmas meal in a basement kitchen and carry it up two flights of stairs."

"It's all right, Greg."

"I just made you a promise, Lil, not a threat. This will be the last Christmas you'll spend like this."

"Greg?"

"Yeah, Lil."

"I got something for you. Under the tree."

"But, Lil, we got all our presents at The Fair."

"This is something special, Greg."

I opened it up. It was a brown leather briefcase with my initials on it. That little brown bag I had always thought the top comics carried. Lil, oh, Lil, how did you ever know?

How we talked that night. She told me how she had done extra typing for graduate students at the University, and she had saved the money. And I told her about old Sally Wells, the lady who owned the Apex Club, the old witch doctor who had predicted I would get married soon and that I'd be flying around the country with a little brown bag. I had never told Lil the story before, never told her about the little brown bag. There was such excitement in her eyes and in her voice.

"Is this it, Greg, is this the bag?"

"Yeah, baby, this is it."

There was no fear in me now, no fear about paying off the television, or paying off The Fair, or supporting my wife, or getting money to take my daughter to the doctor. I couldn't get scared even when there were no jobs for the rest of the year, when January came and there was nothing for me to do. I had me my little brown bag.

On January 13, 1961, my agent called. Irwin Corey, the comic at the Playboy Club, had gotten sick. They needed a replacement that night.

I borrowed a quarter from the landlord downstairs. I took the wrong bus downtown, and it let me off twenty blocks from the Playboy Club. I started to run, and the wind knocked the water out of my eyes, and the cold crawled up my sleeves. They gave me the news at the door. They were very sorry. They hadn't realized that the room had been booked by a convention of frozen food executives from the South. They would give me fifty dollars for the night. They would try to work me in again soon. But they didn't think this would be the best kind of audience to break in with.

If I hadn't been so cold and so mad and so broke, I would have accepted it and gone back home. The room manager was very nice, and maybe he was right. The Playboy Club was a very sophisticated place, the most publicized night club in the country, and a room filled with well-to-do Southerners would be tough to handle. But I was cold and mad and I had run twenty blocks and I didn't even have another quarter to go back home. I told him I was going to do the show they had called me for, I had come too far to stop now. I told him I didn't

care if he had a lynch mob in that room, I was going on
—tonight.

He looked at me and he shrugged. Then he stepped
aside and opened the door to the top.

VI

Good evening, ladies and gentlemen. I understand there are a good many Southerners in the room tonight. I know the South very well. I spent twenty years there one night. . . .

It's dangerous for me to go back. You see, when I drink, I think I'm Polish. One night I got so drunk I moved out of my own neighborhood. . . .

Last time I was down South I walked into this restaurant, and this white waitress came up to me and said: "We don't serve colored people here."

I said: "That's all right, I don't eat colored people. Bring me a whole fried chicken."

About that time these three cousins come in, you know the ones I mean, Klu, Kluck, and Klan, and they say: "Boy, we're givin' you fair warnin'. Anything you do to that chicken, we're gonna do to you." About then the waitress brought me my chicken. "Remember, boy, anything you do to that chicken, we're gonna do to you." So I put down my knife and fork, and I picked up that chicken, and I kissed it.

I went all the way back to childhood that night in the Playboy Club, to the smile Momma always had on her face, to the clever way a black boy learns never to let the bitterness inside him show. The audience fought me with dirty, little, insulting statements, but I was faster, and I was funny, and when that room broke it was like the storm was over. They stopped heckling and they listened. What was supposed to be a fifty-minute show lasted for about an hour and forty minutes. Everytime I tried to get off the stage, they called me back. When I finally said good night, those Southerners stood up and clapped, and when I started toward the door they took money out of their pockets and gave it to me. And one of those Southerners looked at me and said: "You know, if you have the right managers, you'll die a billionaire." It was the greatest compliment I had ever gotten.

Hugh Hefner, the owner of the Playboy Club, caught the second show I gave that night. He signed me to a three-year contract, starting with $250 a week for six weeks in 1961. It was a hell of a thing for people to ask if I was working. I could stick out my chest and say: Yeah, baby, I'm over at the Playboy.

After Hefner hired me, all kinds of things started to happen. I started to get press notices, the newspapers sent people by to review my act, the columnists started quoting my jokes. I'd buy every paper every night, and if I saw my name in one I'd run over to another newsstand to make sure *all* the copies of that newspaper had my name in it. *Time* magazine ran my picture and a rave review. There were calls from agents and managers and night clubs and record companies. The phone never stopped ringing.

I got a lot of help that year. Tim Boxer, the newspaperman I met at The Fickle Pickle, was working hard as my press agent. Associated Booking was getting me jobs. Alex Drier, a big Chicago television personality, invited me by his house to talk about proper management. Alex lived on the Gold Coast of Chicago, and the night I drove out there the police stopped me three times along the way. They figured that any Negro there after dark could only be there to steal. I should have worn a chauffeur's uniform. But it was worth it. When I finally got to his house, Alex was warm and friendly and encouraging and as helpful as usual. He introduced me to Ralph Mann and Marv Josephson, who became my managers. I got lawyers, Dick Shelton and Bernie Kleinman, to handle my account. When you've been busted as long as I had been busted, and suddenly people are waving contracts and money under your nose, you need good, honest, smart businessmen around you. You can't go downtown to wheel and deal for yourself because you aren't used to thinking like a big entertainer with a future; you're still thinking like a guy who is busted.

Then I got a call to come to New York for the "Jack Paar Show." The day I went was a hell of a day. First time I was ever in a jet, first time I ever stayed in a big white hotel. I met Joe Glaser, the head of Associated Booking, a man worth millions. He told me if there was anything I wanted in the hotel, just pick up the phone and call downstairs. His office would take care of the bill. By the time I got on the "Paar Show," so much had happened to me that I wasn't as nervous as I should have been. But it was a hell of a thing to be on national television, on the biggest show in the country, and be allowed to make honest racial jokes right in everybody's living room. Being on the "Jack Paar Show" made me in America.

When I got back from New York, I called Lil from the airport. "Hey, baby, anything done happen in my life?"

"Well, Greg, David Susskind called, he wants you on his show, the Paar people called, they want you back again, and are you ready for the big one?"

"Yeah, baby, lay it on me."

"They just came and repossessed your television set."

"Good. Honey, don't you worry about it."

On the way back home, I stopped at my lawyers' and asked them to get me the biggest color television set on the market.

"How big, Dick?"

"Tell them to go by my apartment and measure the doors. I want the set so big, they got to take all the doors down to get it in the house."

And I told my lawyers to pay off the people who took the other set. Tell them to keep it. They pulled a trick on some poor people. But the trick was on them. They had given me time to pacify my family.

I didn't have to pacify them any more. There were more television shows, and big night-club contracts, and concert offers, and articles about me in national magazines. I bought Lil a Thunderbird for her birthday that

year. I got a kick out of the Thunderbird. Lil didn't
know how to drive, and that Thunderbird just sat out
there in front of that furnished apartment on Wentworth
Avenue. That was getting back at the system.

And then the big one. That August, Lynne Lucille, our
second daughter, was born. In a private hospital.

I was growing by the minute, meeting fascinating people, like Hefner and Paar and Bob Hope. I was flying
first-class to California and New York. One day, one of
the biggest record companies called. They wanted me to
cut a comedy record for them. I was thrilled. I'm sure
I would have done it for them, but the man who came
by to talk to me took me to the wrong restaurant—a
fancy place called London House that scared me to
death. The man ordered lobster tails, so I ordered lobster tails. When the waiter brought the lobster tails, I
realized that I didn't have the slightest idea how to eat
them. So I watched the man from the record company.
He squirted some lemon on his lobster, so I squirted
some lemon on my lobster. But by the time I finished
squirting, he had already taken his first swing at the
tail, and cut it open. I had missed his move, and I didn't
know what to do. So I told him I had an upset stomach,
and I walked out of the restaurant.

But a little while later, Colpix Records offered me a
$25,000 advance for two albums. I took it. That really
tied up a loose end for me, that $25,000 check. I wished
I still had my telegram. I hadn't really told a lie after
all.

There were some other loose ends that got tied up that
year. In May, I went back to Southern Illinois University
with Dizzy Gillespie, for a concert. Doc Lingle was there,
and the dean, and the president. I was a hero again.

And that summer, in San Francisco, I met Big Pres.
We didn't talk very long. There wasn't very much to
say. He was married again, he had other children. He
was working hard and living right. I still felt a lot of
resentment toward him. And I was surprised to find he
was only about my height, five-foot-ten. I had always
thought of him as a giant.

I felt a little sorry for him, too, and I promised him that he was still the grandfather to my children, and that they would visit him. They would give him the respect they would have to give to any grandfather. I didn't see him again that year, but I kept my promise about the children.

That fall, I went to Buffalo for an engagement, and after a show a guy came up and said there was a lady who wanted to see me. For some reason I knew immediately who it was. I knew she had been living in Buffalo for some years, and I was so nervous that I went back to my dressing room to smoke and go to the bathroom before I went to her table. And when I sat down and looked at her, I found out that when a man waits for something and begs for something and prays for something for twenty-two years, from the time he's seven years old until he's twenty-nine, that thing just doesn't qualify any more. No, I didn't want Helene Tucker any more. I was after a *Helena,* and I had her at home and her name was Lillian.

That was a big year, 1961. Made it to the top, and found my Daddy and found Helene Tucker, and wiped out that $25,000 lie. I came off the road in November, back to Chicago, thinking how I was going to wrap up this beautiful year in a final beautiful package. I had me a brilliant idea, and I schemed out one hell of a plot.

A friend of mine, an interior decorator, was in on the trick. We went and found an apartment in the Hyde Park section, an integrated building near the University. I told him to take that apartment and spare no expense. I want to move in on Christmas morning, and the only thing I want to take with me from the furnished apartment on Wentworth is the color television set, so I could watch them tear the doors down again. I want this place to be perfect. I want to walk in here on Christmas morning and start living in it, I want to open up that new refrigerator and cook ham and eggs.

He did a hell of a job, went and bought furniture and

carpeting and drapes, and when I went back I nearly flipped. I couldn't believe we were going to live in anything so beautiful. Now I brought my lawyer in on the trick. Three days before Christmas, I had him call Lil. He was supposed to tell her I was having trouble with my income tax. The Internal Revenue had taken every penny I had made for the entire year. We were broke again. I lay there in bed that morning, listening to Lil talk to him over the phone. I lay there waiting for her to come in and give me the bad news. And I waited. Finally, I couldn't stay in bed, any more.

"Anybody call me while I was sleeping, Lil?"

"No, Greg."

"But I heard the phone ring."

"Oh, it was just the lawyer."

"What about?"

"He didn't tell me."

I called him back, and asked why he hadn't given Lil the message. He said he had.

When you have that *Helena* you're just not going to hear any bad news from her lips. Nothing sounds bad to her when you're around.

"Lil?"

"Yeah, Greg?"

"We're going to have to sell the toys we bought the kids, and we're going to have to give your car back."

"That's okay, Greg."

"Baby, I'm sorry but it's going to be the worst Christmas we ever had."

"Don't worry about anything, Greg, we'll be all right."

I had planned to stage a big eviction scene, but just looking at all that peace and trust in her face, I canceled that plan out.

There were still a lot of things that had to go into the new apartment that nobody but Lil could buy. So two days before Christmas, I told her that a friend of mine had called to ask if we could help out a young couple who had just moved to Chicago. The couple had some money, but no credit in town. Since the stores probably didn't know yet that Dick Gregory was busted, we could open a charge account in our name for them, and we could help them buy their furnishings. Lillian said she'd be glad to help them.

We spent all that day shopping with this couple Lil didn't know. Lil helped that woman pick out dishes and silverware and sheets and bedspreads and towels as carefully as if she were picking them out for herself. And somehow, Lil never caught on to the clever way that other woman made sure Lil liked something before she charged it. When we left the store, we had about ten cabs full of stuff, plus my car and my friend's car. I sent Lil home in another cab, and we took the stuff to the new apartment.

We had no tree Christmas Eve, no toys for the kids, no gifts for each other. I told Lil I couldn't take her to the club with me that night because I couldn't afford to run my tab up. But after the show, I picked her up and carried her to a party in the Hyde Park section given by a big Chicago columnist, Tony Weitzel, and his wife, Carmen. He was in on the trick. Lil was fascinated by Tony's apartment.

"If you really want to see something, Lil," said Tony, "let me show you what one of these apartments looks like brand new." He took a bunch of us up to the ninth floor.

Lil walked in that door, and it was beautiful to see the way her face lit up. "Oh, it's lovely, it's so fine. Those people will be so happy in here."

She walked around and looked at the apartment, and her face was so full of happiness I almost cried. She was being happy for somebody else.

Then she noticed some of the things she had bought in the store two days before, and she grabbed my arm. "Greg, oh, Greg . . ."

And her eyes got wide, and her mouth fell open, and she saw one of Michele's toys underneath the Christmas tree in the middle of the living-room floor. Lillian screamed, and she fainted.

That was Christmas, 1961, so different from all the

Christmases I'd ever had. It was as if I had rolled it all together in one big ball, and bounced it, and while it was up in the air, said:

It's get-even time, Santa.

VII

And suddenly you wake up one morning with a smirky smile because you're standing on the other side of that plate-glass window and you say: Damn, this wasn't hard, this wasn't hard at all. In January, 1961, you were putting cardboard in your shoes to keep out the cold, and in 1962 you have more shoes than you'll ever wear. You buy suits like jelly beans. You can take your kids to the doctor *before* they get sick. You play a show on Broadway. You take your wife to Hawaii for a vacation. Baby, you got it made in the shade.

But the old monster is still hanging around, he's not satisfied yet. You got to work for him, too. You take twenty-one juvenile delinquents on a road trip to Detroit to let them meet Walter Reuther and the governor and have a dance with some local Helene Tuckers, and get a little dignity. You make those night-club owners advertise in Negro papers in cities where they advertise in the white press and there is also a Negro press, and you put a nonsegregation clause in your contract. You start doing a lot of benefit shows for CORE and the NAACP. You start doing shows in prisons.

Two of those shows I'll never forget as long as I live. The one that scared me the most—physically—was at the Maryland State Penitentiary. Until I walked into that cellblock, I had no idea the prison was segregated. The white prisoners were sitting in the middle, and the Negro prisoners were sitting on the sides. I told the priest who had brought me in that I had never worked in front of a segregated audience and I wouldn't start now. He told me that the prisoners had been waiting for my show all week, and that if I didn't go on there would be a riot. I

152

told him to integrate the seats and I'd go on. He went and got the warden.

The warden said there would be a riot if I didn't go on. He said that the convicts had been sitting that way for thirty-two years, and he couldn't do anything about it. He told me that for the first time in history they had let the Death Row prisoners out to watch a show. They were in the balcony.

"Let me out the back door, warden. Tell the boys I had a heart attack."

He begged me to go on. He promised me if I did this show, the very next one they had would be integrated. But that monster was jumping, that dry taste, that hot water seeping up.

"Okay, man, you say if you try to integrate them there'll be a riot, and if I don't go on there'll be a riot. Tell you what. Either I can walk out that back door, and never give it a second thought, or I can go out there and try to integrate them. That way, at least I'll be here to get killed with you."

The last thing I heard before I went out on the stage was that priest's voice. "Do it with humor," he was saying. "Do it with humor."

It seemed like a mile out to that microphone, and I was petrified all the way. There were 1,200 men in that room, and now that I was in front of them I'd never get to that back door if this thing rips. If anything happens, I'm dead. And the papers will say it was my jokes that incited a race riot.

"Gentlemen, I've worked many pens before, and believe me when I tell you I enjoy entertaining you fellows. But I want to tell you we have a problem here today."

They were looking at me, puzzled. Out of the corner of my eye, I could see the warden whispering into a telephone.

"I've never worked before a segregated audience and I don't intend to. Now, if you fellows want one hell of a show, I want to see you switch those seats."

I'm waiting for it to happen now, and my eyes are half closed, and I'm wondering whether the white cons are going to bust first, or if the Negro cons are going to take offense for me and bust first. And then there's screaming and hollering and a white man in the front row jumps up and walks to the side and a Negro con yells, "Thank God, baby," and they're switching seats. Not all of them, a lot of the white men never moved, but that morning I saw five white prisoners lifting a crippled old Negro to the center row, and I saw smiles on black and white faces as they got up and changed their seats.

Now back to the show, hit them quick. I look down at that beautiful white guy who made the first move. "Hey, baby, I dig integration and all that, but I still don't know if I'd give up that good seat."

They were laughing now and I poured it on for forty-five minutes, strictly racial material because I didn't want to let them relax for a minute, but I wanted them to know what had happened. After the show, I was scared again when I realized how close it had been. Most of the audience gave me a standing ovation, but there were a lot of white men who wouldn't even look at me when I went down on the floor to shake hands.

As I was leaving, the priest tried to apologize in his own way. "There's a lot of good white people in America, Dick. All the white folks in the South aren't bad. It's just going to take time and education."

"Father, they're the same kind of people who crucified Christ. And you stand there and defend them? Impossible."

But it was the show at the Michigan State Penitentiary that really scared me—in a different way. It had been a good show—prison audiences are so hungry for entertainment. As I came off the stage, the warden introduced me to an old Negro who had been in jail for fifty years. He was an artist, and he asked me if I'd like to see his work. I did. When I saw it I got weak in the knees.

He had drawings of women, of what he thought women looked like. But every one had a man's face, a man's eyes, a man's nose, a man's jaw, a man's lips. They had long hair and they had breasts and they were wearing lipstick and dresses. But every one was really a man.

It was so weird that a man should think he was drawing a woman and he was really drawing a man. But that convict had seen only men for fifty years; those male faces were all he knew. And I talked to Lil about it and the more we talked and the more I thought about it, the more frightened I got. If you had told that old man that his drawings were all wrong he would have called you a liar and been ready to fight. And then Lil and I carried it one step further. If you were born and raised in America, and hate and fear and racial prejudice are all you've ever known, if they're all you've ever seen . . .

I kept thinking about that old convict all that year. It was a big year, a busy year. San Francisco, New York, Los Angeles, Las Vegas, the sophisticated supper clubs, the big one-night concerts. More publicity, more television, more magazine articles. Went back and did some free shows for some of the people who helped me along the way, laid some bread on those cats who gave me money when I needed it. And I kept pushing my material further, more topical, more racial, more digging into a system I was beginning to understand better and attack more intelligently. I was speaking at more and more rallies and benefits now, getting to know and talk with the civil rights leaders—Roy Wilkins, Whitney Young, James Farmer, Martin Luther King—beginning to realize just how large and complicated this problem is. I was learning that just being a Negro doesn't qualify you to understand the race situation any more than being sick makes you an expert on medicine.

When I was in San Francisco that year, a civil rights leader asked me to come over to Oakland and speak before a rally of a thousand Negro plum-pickers. I told them I'd be glad to. He offered me some literature. I refused it. What did I need literature for? I could talk before any group about racial problems. But I was wrong. What could I tell these people about migratory workers taking their jobs away? What could I tell them about their women being forced to climb too high on plum-picking ladders? Their problems were racial, and yet they weren't racial, they were geographical, and yet they affected all Negroes. And could the plum-pickers fully understand the Negroes who wanted to be allowed to try on hats and shoes in the department stores of Birmingham?

That fall, Medgar Evers called and asked me to speak at the voter registration rallies in Jackson, Mississippi. When he told me that the Jackson NAACP headquarters was on Lynch Street, I felt a little nervous. But I told him I'd be down just as soon as I could make the time.

I was afraid of the South, afraid of all the cities where I could fall down accidentally, break my head open, and be left to bleed to death in the gutter because the ambulance from the Negro funeral home had to come all the way across town.

VIII

In November of 1962 I was sitting on the stage of a jam-packed auditorium in Jackson, Mississippi, with Roy Wilkins, waiting to go on. I was a little restless. I had flown in just for that night, and I wanted to make my speech and get out of town. And now I had to sit up there and wait while they were introducing some old Negro who had just gotten out of jail. I hardly listened. He had killed a man, they said, another Negro who had been sent by the whites to burn the old man's house down. The old man had been leading a voter registration drive. I should have listened carefully. But I had no way of knowing that old man was going to change my entire life.

The old man shuffled out to the microphone. I think he said he was seventy-eight years old. I'll never forget what he said next.

"I didn't mind going to jail for freedom, no, I wouldn't even mind being killed for freedom. But my wife and I was married a long time, and, well, you know I ain't never spent a night away from home. While I was in jail, my wife died."

That destroyed me. I sat there, and my stomach turned around, and I couldn't have stood up if I had to. Here's this little old Mississippi Negro, the kind of big-lipped, kinky-haired, black-faced verb-buster every other Negro in America looks down on. And this man bucked and rose up and fought the system for me, and he went to jail for me, and he lost his wife for me. He had gone out on the battle lines and demonstrated for a tomorrow he would never see, for jobs and rights he might not even be qualified to benefit from. A little old man from

157

a country town who never spent a night away from his
wife in his married life. And he went to jail for me and
being away killed her.

After the old man finished speaking, I went to him
and told him thanks. I told him that I hated to come to
him with money after what had happened to him, but if
he had a child or loved one anywhere in the world he
wanted to see on Christmas, I wanted the privilege of
sending him there. He said he had a son in California,
and later I gave Medgar Evers a train ticket and a check
for the old man.

I don't remember what I spoke about that night, I was
so upset. As I came off the stage, Medgar introduced me
to a woman named Leona Smith as if I should know her.
When I didn't react, he said she was the mother of Clyde
Kennard. That name didn't mean anything to me either.
So Medgar told me a story that made me sick.

Clyde Kennard was thirty-five years old, and for the
past three years he had been in jail. The charge was stealing five bags of chicken feed. But the real reason was
that he had tried to enroll in Mississippi Southern College. Before I left Jackson that night, I promised Mrs.
Smith that I would do everything in my power to get her
son out of jail. When I got back to Chicago, Medgar
started calling me about the case and sending me more
information. I couldn't believe it.

Kennard was born in Mississippi, and he attended the
University of Chicago. When he got out of the para-
troopers after Korea, he bought his parents a farm in
Mississippi. His stepfather got sick, and Clyde went down
to run the farm. He wanted to finish his college education, so in 1959 he applied to the nearest school,
Mississippi Southern. He was turned down and harassed
by the police, and finally somebody planted five stolen
bags of chicken feed on his farm. The price of feed was
raised to make the charge a felony, and Kennard was
sentenced to seven years at hard labor. When another
Negro admitted stealing the feed, the white authorities
told him to shut up.

On New Year's Eve, from the stage of Mister Kelley's

in Chicago, I made a resolution for 1963: Get Kennard out of jail. I thought that if all the facts were dug up and printed in the newspapers, America would get Kennard out of jail. A white UPI reporter who came by to interview me was so upset by the story that he volunteered to go into Mississippi and gather more information. The first bit of information he dug up was that Clyde Kennard was dying of cancer.

Irv Kupcinet, the famous Chicago columnist, broke the Kennard story. My new researcher came up with Kennard's medical records, and gave them to the press. Kennard was transferred to the prison hospital. Then a Chicago millionaire called business connections in Mississippi, and Kennard was released from jail. He was thirty-five years old when we flew him to Chicago to start cancer treatments, but he looked eighty-five. And it was too late. He died six months later.

I met James Meredith that year, too—one of the most brilliant and courageous men in America, a man who gave dignity to every Negro in the country, who put every Negro in college, who played one of the biggest parts in setting up the revolution in the history of the American Negro struggle. Negroes looked a little different and acted a little different when James Meredith was graduated because they all were graduated with him, graduated from the derogatory stigma that all Negroes are ignorant, that all Negroes are lazy, that all Negroes stink.

I was different, too. An old man's wife had died. Two young men had tried to integrate schools that the biggest fools wouldn't want to go to. One had failed and died, and the other had succeeded and suffered. For the first time, I was involved. There was a battle going on, there was a war shaping up, and somehow writing checks and giving speeches didn't seem enough.

Made in the shade? Hell, as long as any man, white or black, isn't getting his rights in America I'm in danger. Sure I could stay in the night clubs and say clever things. But if America goes to war tomorrow would I stay home and satirize it at the Blue Angel? No, I'd go overseas and

lay on some cold dirt, taking the chance of dying to
guarantee a bunch of foreigners a better life than my
own Momma got in America.

I wanted a piece of the action now, I wanted to get in
this thing. I got my chance sooner than I expected.

Some people in Mississippi were having problems with
food. A guy came by the night club one evening in Chicago and asked me to sign a fund-raising letter. I told him
I never lend my name to anything. If it's an organization
I can work with, I'll work. I told him I didn't get through
at the night club until 4 A.M. but if he'd leave some literature under my apartment door I'd read it before I went
to sleep. He did. I got another lesson on how dirty this
situation was.

Leflore County in Mississippi had cut off its shipments
of federal surplus foods, most of which went to Negroes.
This was in retaliation for voter registration drives in
Greenwood, the county seat. The white authorities claimed
they couldn't afford the $37,000 a year it cost them to
store and distribute the free food to the poor people. I
endorsed the letter that morning and sent a check for
$100.

Later that day, the fund-raisers called me and asked
if I would come by for a press conference. I asked for
more information so I could answer questions intelligently. And I sent my new researcher down to Greenwood.
Then I went into the streets of Chicago. Daddy-O Day-
ley, the disc jockey, and I collected 14,000 pounds of
food. I chartered a plane, and on February 11, 1963,
we flew the food into Memphis. We loaded it into trucks
there, and drove 134 miles to Clarksdale. From there
it was taken to Greenwood. I was still afraid of the
South, and I wanted to leave that night. That's why I
picked February 11 to go to Mississippi. The next day
was Lincoln's Birthday and President Kennedy had invited Lil and me and 800 other people to a celebration
at the White House. So we handed out the food, and I
promised the voter registration workers from SNCC—
the Student Non-Violent Coordinating Committee—that
I'd come back when the demonstrations began. Then I

headed back to Memphis, flew to Chicago to pick up Lil, and flew on to Washington.

It was a wonderful affair. We shook hands with President Kennedy, and with Lyndon Johnson. Lil was almost nine months pregnant at the time, and I was hoping she'd give birth right in the White House. Waited around as long as we could, but the party was over and she didn't even feel labor pains. So we went back to Chicago.

I started getting reports from my researcher. Through February and March there was violence in Greenwood. Cars were wrecked, a Negro registration worker was shot in the back of the neck, the SNCC headquarters was set on fire. Bullets were fired into Negro homes. SNCC workers were beaten up. When Negroes marched in protest, the police put the dogs on them. They arrested the eleven top registration workers. And I had promised to go down to Greenwood.

I was scared to death. Making speeches, giving money, even going down South for a night or two at a time—that was one thing. But getting out on those streets and marching against bullets and dogs and water hoses and cattle prods . . .

I knew they were laying for me down there. The Mississippi newspapers and public officials were on me for the food lift. They claimed that I hadn't brought down 14,000 pounds of food after all, that it had been much less. They said that if Dick Gregory was going to take care of their poor Negroes, let's send them all up to Chicago. They said I was just doing it for publicity.

And then the time came to make up my mind. The big push for voter registration was scheduled to start on April 1. Most of the SNCC people were in jail, and they needed leaders in Greenwood. And they needed a well-known name that would bring the situation national attention. On Sunday, March 31, I lay on a hotel bed in Philadelphia and changed my mind a hundred times. I thought of a lot of good reasons for not going.

They'll kill me down there, those rednecks, they'll call me an outside agitator and pull me into an alley and beat my head in, they'll shoot me down in the street.

What's that going to prove? And what about Michele and Lynne and Lil, lying in a hospital right now with Dick, Jr., my son, who's going to grow up with nothing but some press clippings for a Daddy?

If Whitey down South doesn't kill me in Greenwood, then Whitey up North will kill me in show business. Everybody I talked to but Lil told me not to go. It would ruin me as a comic. Nobody's going to come to laugh at an entertainer who goes marching and demonstrating and getting himself arrested.

I had two airline tickets in my room, one for me and one for James Sanders, a brilliant young Negro comedy writer. I dropped them in the wastebasket. I'll call SNCC headquarters, tell them I'm sick, I've changed my mind, I can't break my contract and leave town. I called Lil instead, at the hospital. She told me not to worry about anything, to go down if I wanted to, and suddenly I was telling her about that Mississippi Negro, the man that other Negroes called nigger, that cotton-picker in his tarpaper shack who could rip this thing, who could give courage to every Negro in America, who could wake up the nation. I had faith then that when America saw what was happening in Greenwood, it would make sure that it never happened again, anywhere. I wanted to be a part of this thing, but I was scared.

Sure, I had made speeches that every door of racial prejudice I can kick down is one less door that my children have to kick down. But, hell, my kids don't have to worry. . . .

I lay there all that night, into the morning, going, not going, picking the tickets out of the wastebasket, throwing them back in, but never tearing them up. And as I lay there my own life started spinning around in my mind, and my stomach turned over, and I thought about St. Louis and Momma and Richard, running off to buy himself a dinner of a Twinkie Cupcake and a bottle of Pepsi-Cola, little Richard whose Daddy was so broken by the system that he ran away and came back just to take the rent money out of the jar in the kitchen. Goddamn, we're always running and hiding, and then I thought about an old man whose wife had died, and about Clyde Kennard, and about James Meredith, they didn't run away, and now it was almost dawn in Philadelphia and there was a familiar dry taste in my mouth, and that old hot water was seeping into a cold body and my room was the grandstand of the biggest stadium in the world—America—and the race was for survival and the monster said go.

One Less Door

I

"What are you going to do if they spit in your face, if they hit you, if they knock you down?" an old man asked me. "You going to hit back?"

"I'm going to try not to."

The old man shook his head. "We can't use you."

"You can't use me? Why the hell not?"

"Mister Gregory, you got to *know* you're not going to fight back."

I couldn't believe I was standing on a Greenwood street and listening to an old Mississippi Negro, a man I had come down to do a favor for, tell me he can't use me. I told him I'd have to think about it. He nodded his nappy old head and said he'd be back, and shuffled away.

I thought about it, and the more I thought the more I realized how beautiful this thing really was. It was my second day in Greenwood. Monday morning, Jim Sanders and I had caught the eight o'clock flight from New York to Memphis. The plane was filled. I didn't find out why until we landed and a man came over and said he was from the Department of Justice.

"How long are you going to be here, Mister Gregory?"

"I'm not staying in Memphis. I'm going on to Greenwood."

"I know that. We have orders to stay until you leave."

A SNCC car picked us up and drove us to Greenwood. The press was there, the national magazines, the national television networks. They all asked me how long I was going to stay because they had to stay as long as I did. I couldn't believe it. Just for me. I didn't know, until I got to Greenwood, that the SNCC kids had announced to the press that I was expected.

167

There were no demonstrations that first day, but I spoke at a crowded church rally that night. First I answered all the charges that the local newspapers and public officials had made against me. I told them if they didn't believe I had brought 14,000 pounds of food, they should check the records of Delta Air Lines. I told them that they weren't just dealing with Dick Gregory when they threatened to take all the Negroes off relief, they were dealing with America. They weren't big enough to threaten the whole country. And I'd be glad to take a lie detector test if the governor thought I was doing all this for publicity.

Then I got on the Negro church. There were fifteen Negro churches in Greenwood, and only two of them had opened their doors to the demonstrators. I stood up there and told that crowd how the Negro preachers had brought us all the way to the battle lines and then had abandoned us. They were scared of losing their jobs, of having their churches bombed, of coming up empty in their collection plates. Our church was failing us in this battle for civil rights. It was the preachers' fault that whenever we made a gain we said: "Thank the United States Supreme Court," instead of saying "Thank God."

I looked at those people in that church, those beautiful people who were taking chances with their lives, with what little they had in the world. There wasn't a single Negro doctor in Greenwood. When Negroes demonstrate they forfeit their medical attention. A Negro couldn't even afford to get sick. And they were going out, maybe to die, without any of their local Negro leaders. The preachers were scared, and the Negro schoolteachers and principals were too afraid for their jobs to go out in the streets. That night, standing in front of those people, I told them I'd be proud to lead them in demonstrations the next day. I really hadn't planned to lead the marching, but looking at those beautiful faces ready to die for freedom, I knew I couldn't do less.

It was the next morning, while we were getting ready to march on the courthouse, that the old man came up to me. We were standing in front of the SNCC headquarters, about fifty of us and dozens of press and television people, when he told me he couldn't use me. By the time he came back again, my anger was gone. I understood what he meant.

"We're ready to go, Mister Gregory, what do you think?"

"Okay, I'll do it."

So we marched. Old people, kids, voter registration workers, women. We marched for one block, and every step of the way I was scared, waiting for that bullet to come from a rooftop, waiting for that car to come by and shoot me from the ground.

The police stopped us after one block and told us we couldn't parade through the city. So we jumped into cars, made the two-mile trip to the courthouse, and reassembled. We caught the cops off-guard. They closed the courthouse early that day so no Negroes could register to vote. We started walking away in small groups, and suddenly there was a hand on my stomach and I heard a cop say: "I oughta kill him," and the next thing I knew someone had twisted my arm behind my back and was pushing me across the street. It was a Greenwood policeman.

"Move on, nigger."

"Thanks a million."

"Thanks for what?"

"Up North police don't escort me across the street against a red light."

"I said, move on, nigger."

"I don't know my way, I'm new in this town."

The cop yanked on my arm and turned his head. "Send someone over to show this nigger where to go," he hollered.

They were pushing the marchers around, dozens of regular policemen and auxiliary policemen with clubs and guns, and the press and the cameramen moved in and out of the crowds of white men and women and children standing on the street corners. I pulled one of my arms free and pointed at the crowd.

"Ask that white woman over there to come here and show me where to go."

The cop's face got red, and there was spittle at the corner of his mouth. All he could say was: "Nigger, dirty nigger . . ."

I looked at him. "Your momma's a nigger. Probably got more Negro blood in her than I could ever hope to have in me."

He dropped my other arm then, and backed away, and his hand was on his gun. I thought he was going to explode. But nothing happened. I was sopping wet and too excited to be scared. We walked on back to the headquarters, the police yelling and shoving and harassing us all the way. We decided to march again that afternoon.

I learned a lot that day. I felt the poisonous hate in an American city, a nice-looking little town that had a Confederate flag flying just as high as the American flag on the U.S. Post Office. I saw the beauty of those college kids from SNCC, day and night, around the clock, hardly ever sleeping or eating as they sat in hot and dirty rooms teaching old Negroes how to read and write so they could pass the voting tests. And I saw the Southern white man who has nothing between him and the lowest Negro except a segregated toilet. No wonder so many of them have shithouse ways.

When we started back to the courthouse late that afternoon, a skinny old woman who said she was ninety-eight years old came up to me. "Mister Gregory, you be embarrassed if I walk downtown with you, me and my snuff box? I want to come down and be with you today. I don't mind dyin'."

And so we marched again.

Demonstrating in the South must be a little like being in a battle in a war. There's noise and confusion and pushing and quick huddles over strategy and running back and forth on both sides. You're never really sure of what's happening. You see snatches of things, hear sounds, you keep moving long after you're exhausted because you're too excited to know how tired you are.

There are little victories that make you feel good for a while. That afternoon, we changed our route to the courthouse, and instead of marching through the center of town we cut through a white neighborhood. It took the police almost a half-hour to catch up with us.

"Dirty nigger."

"Your mother's a nigger," I told the cop.

"Damn black monkey."

"Who you calling a monkey? Monkey's got thin lips, monkey's got blue eyes and straight hair."

"Just keep movin', boy, just keep movin'. . . ."

The police seemed disorganized. They tried to break us up again and one of them shoved a woman pretty hard. She stumbled and smashed her head against a brick wall and fell on the sidewalk. One of the SNCC workers couldn't stand that, and he turned on the cop. They dragged him off into a police car, and five cops climbed in after him and started working on his head and stomach. One of the cops was saying in a loud voice, mostly for the benefit of the other demonstrators: "George, gimme ma knife. . . . I'm gonna cut the balls right off this little nigger, he ain't never gonna do nothin' no more."

Now I was at the head of the line and I refused to move an inch until they brought the SNCC kid back. Two cops grabbed me and threw me into the back of a police car. One of them asked the driver: "You want any help with this nigger?"

"Why you always think a Negro's going to hurt somebody? Close the door and let this fool take me to jail."

He slammed the door and walked away.

The cop who was driving turned around and started slapping at my head. I held my hands up over my face.

"Get your hands down, nigger," he yelled and kept swinging at my head. He didn't do much damage. Then he started the car and drove about three blocks, away from everything. He pulled the car over to the curb, and when he turned around again he was crying.

"My God, what are you trying to do to me?"

He sat in that car and he looked at me and he told me

that when he went home at night his kids looked at him funny, that they made him feel bad. I sat there, and I couldn't believe I was hearing these words from a white cop who had been hitting me and niggering me a few minutes before. He said: "As right as you are, you're down here helping these people and I got to stop you and I can't and sometimes I think you're a better man than I am."

He didn't take me to jail. He drove me back to registration headquarters. I got out of the car and handed him two dollars.

"What's this for?"

"I always tip chauffeurs. Hell, if you don't take me to jail, you're my chauffeur."

I got into a SNCC car and rushed back to the demonstration. When I climbed out, the police commissioner, Hammond, came right over.

"Boy, what you come back here for?"

"Hammond, anytime you arrest me you better carry me to jail because if you don't that's kidnapping and that's a federal offense."

A little cop came over. "Nigger, you want to go to jail."

I said: "Come here, boy, let me tell you something. I could take you to Chicago today and let you walk through my home, then come back here and walk through your home, and out of the two of us you'd know which one was the nigger."

Then the cops turned their backs and walked away, leaving us there on the corner. The parade was over and we did exactly what they had been screaming at us to do—we broke up into twos and threes and went in different directions.

That night, Jim Sanders and I drove fifty miles to a mass meeting in Clarksdale. There were more than 800 people jammed into the Centennial Missionary Baptist Church there, and we had to push our way through the police to get inside. I was sitting on the stage, waiting to speak, when the bomb came flying through an open window. It hit a man on the head, bounced off a lady's hand, then rolled to the middle of the floor.

I just sat there, frightened, and saw my wife and my kids and everything decent in my life and wondered why I was sitting here, fixing to die and leave all that, and it flashed through my mind that it was worth it. When I looked up, I saw the reporters and the photographers standing still, writing in their notebooks and taking their pictures while hundreds of Negroes around them were on their feet running for the door. I jumped up and grabbed the microphone.

"Where are you going? The man who threw it is outside God's house. The Man who's supposed to save you lives here."

They stopped in their tracks. Somebody picked up the bomb and threw it back out the window.

I walked outside the church after a while, and looked at the cops lounging around outside, leaning on the hoods of their cars in the evening, talking softly and laughing. I walked across the street and into a Negro grocery store to make a phone call. The police commissioner was in there. He didn't know who I was yet.

"Hey, boy, come over here."

"Yes, sir."

"You just come from the church, huh? That Gregory's in there. He funny, boy?"

"How could any man be funny when a dumb superintendent of police lets these heathen cops do the things they do?"

He got red and walked out. I went back to the church. We found out that the bomb had been a special U.S. Army gas grenade, more powerful than tear gas, which could have killed the people nearby had it gone off. Whoever threw the bomb forgot to pull the pin. And people were surprised a few months later when they blew up that church in Birmingham.

We held our meeting and I spoke. The Clarksdale Negroes weren't as responsive as the Greenwood Negroes because they were more scared of the police, of losing their jobs. And they were all pretty shook up by the grenade. When the meeting was over, a man came in to tell me that I was going to be killed that night. A roadblock had been set up for me on the highway back to Greenwood. The messenger was a Negro, but he said he had been sent by the police commissioner.

Outside the church I could hear one of the police officers screaming, almost hysterical. "If one of our men threw that bomb you'd better believe it would have gone off, we don't make mistakes like that, no, sir, we don't. Our boys don't miss, no we don't."

The folks from the church made a ring around Jim Sanders and me and took us around the corner. We ducked into the drugstore owned by Aaron Henry, the powerful Negro leader, and lay there for an hour until a car was brought up to the back door. Jim and I crouched in the back of the car, and we were taken to the home of a Clarksdale Negro.

We didn't sleep that night, lying on the floor of the house, keeping away from the windows. The Negro had a telephone, and we weren't sure just how afraid he was, and who he was afraid of. We stayed awake to make sure nobody used that phone that night. In the morning, we were driven back to Greenwood along side roads.

They knocked down that ninety-eight-year-old lady that day, right in the streets, and I'll never forget the way she looked up at me from the gutter, her head bleeding. "Don't let them make you mad, honey. They ain't after me, it's you they after."

They arrested Jim that day, the first time he ever went to jail. I told the press I thought it was a good experience for him, make him a better writer. But I was worried, he's such a sweet, patient, good-natured man. They hauled eighteen other Negroes away, bouncing one kid along the pavement, slamming another down on the floor of a bus. They grabbed the Reverend Robert Kinloch so hard his collar came off. One cop threw his club at a registration worker who was taking pictures. It only hit his shoulder. And the police were on their best behavior that day because there were FBI agents in town with movie cameras.

They wouldn't arrest me. Shoved me a little and

pushed me around some, and got mad when I started bad-mouthing Hammond, but they had decided that putting me in jail would bring too much publicity. One cop came up to me and spat right in my face. I started to jump him, but I remembered what I had promised the old man and I held myself back. Just stood there and let the spit run down my face and into my mouth.

"I guess that makes me as white as you now, boy. I got your spit inside me."

It was another long day. I called Lil, who had just come home from the hospital, and told her to take the first plane on down. I wanted her to see the beauty of this Southern Negro, the old people learning to read and write, young and old marching, the women cooking all day so there would always be food ready on the chance a demonstrator might run in for a bite to eat. Lil said she'd be down by morning.

That third day in Greenwood—Wednesday—turned into night and I was alone and scared. You never know what fear is until you walk through the streets of a quiet town at night and it suddenly dawns on you that if anyone attacked you, you couldn't even call the police. You know if you tripped on a curb and broke your ankle, when the ambulance pulled up and found out who you were it would drive away. Or run you over. It's a feeling that takes all the guts out of you.

And on you walk and pace the streets because you have no place to sleep. You're afraid to go into a Negro home. They might see you go in there and blow the house up and you have no right to take a chance with someone else's family. Or it might be the house of a very scared Negro and he might tell them where you are.

And I thought about St. Louis and how we used to rap for Mister Roosevelt every night, and how he once said that there was nothing to fear but fear itself, and I said: "Bullshit." Out loud. Sometimes it makes you feel a little better to talk to the dark. "Bullshit."

I walked around a corner with my head down and when I looked up I saw one of the most vicious white men I ever saw in my life, a big, fat man with a bald head and tobacco juice running out of his mouth. He swung that double-barreled shotgun like it was a toy. It was no toy. He stuck it right into my stomach.

"I'm going to blow your black nigger guts out."

And I was too tired and too gut-scared to move. Then I felt that goddamned monster rise up and I looked in his eye.

"Is that all you plan to do, boy, just kill me? Pull that fucking trigger, boy, you just pull that fucking trigger."

And that no-good dirty mother-fucker was so hung up on his hate weed that he lowered his shotgun and turned and walked away. He just couldn't do anything a Negro told him to do.

On Thursday and Friday I marched with Lil. To the cops, she was just another demonstrator, another face in the crowd. A lot of people said I was crazy to have her come down, but I wanted to share this thing with her, I wanted her to see this beauty and ugliness. We stayed in the home of Reverend Tucker. The police harassment picked up, and the television people started asking us to demonstrate early so they could make the six o'clock news with their film clips. As it turned out, we didn't do much more demonstrating. When the police began taking pictures of the marchers, I turned the group back. The police would use the pictures to permanently blackball and harass the local Negroes, and I didn't want that to happen. They would have to stay in Greenwood long after we left.

I left Greenwood on Saturday morning, April 6. Things had quieted down. Deals had been made. The demonstrators were released from jail, and the city promised to supply the Negroes with buses so they wouldn't walk through town on their way to the courthouse to register. In return, a federal injunction against local harassment was dropped and I promised to leave town. I had learned a lot and I felt so much stronger now; less afraid, like a soldier who has been through his first battle.

A lot happened down there that I'll never know about, a lot happened that I can't talk about now because this war is still going on. And when I got back North, a lot happened that scared me all over again, in a different way.

I found out, for example, that some of the Northern press had reported that the bomb in Clarksdale was only a football bladder. And some had reported that we had lost in Greenwood, and I had played the fool. I knew it couldn't have been the newsmen who had been down there, but it was editors up North who turned and twisted the stories that were sent to them.

But what scared me most was when Negroes asked me if it was true that I had gone down to Greenwood for publicity.

And it dawned on me that anytime you help a Negro in America, even the Negroes will question your intentions. I could have quit show business and joined the Peace Corps and gone to Vietnam and no one, white or black, would have questioned why I did it. But to help Negroes . . .

I was just beginning to realize what a long hard row it would be.

II

It's a great thing to go to jail for right, but whether you're there for right or wrong, when you hear that big steel door close and that key turn, you know you're there. That was Birmingham, May of 1963. Martin Luther King asked me to come down. I arrived at 11:30 A.M. on a Monday, and an hour and a half later I went to jail with more than 800 other demonstrators. It was my first time in jail to stay.

"You Dick Gregory?"

"I'm Mister Gregory."

Somebody snatched my collar and my feet didn't hit the floor again until I was in solitary confinement.

Later in the afternoon I was brought downstairs and put in a cell built for twenty-five people. There must have been 500 of us in there. When they moved us out to eat, the corridors were so crowded you couldn't walk. Just stand still and let the crowd move you along. The last one back in the cell didn't have a place to lie down and sleep.

There was a little boy, maybe four years old, standing in the corner of the cell sucking his thumb. I felt sorry for him. He didn't even have someone his age to play with. I kind of rubbed his head and asked him how he was.

"All right," he said.

"What are you here for?"

"Teedom," he said. Couldn't even say Freedom but he was in jail for it.

The older kids sang church songs, sitting and waiting for the night to pass away. None of us knew how long we were going to be in jail. We were hoping new people would come in with information about the movement outside. We didn't really know, squatting there in that Birmingham jail, that the first really great battle of the revolution was going on outside. That a man named Bull Connor was becoming a symbol to the world of how low and vicious and stupid one American could be to another. That an Alabama city was becoming a symbol to the world of the cancer eating away at our country. On the other side of that wall were dogs and fire hoses and guns and clubs, and the blood of black men and white men, good men and bad men of both colors, and children and women and old people. We were in the battle, but the rest of the world, outside that jail, saw more than we did. Bombs and soldiers and killings. And some of them outside were horrified that Martin Luther King used little children, and some of them understood that Freedom was for little black children, too, that in an all-out war for survival there are no civilians. There were little children in Hiroshima.

The jailers fed us in the morning, and it tasted good because some of us hadn't eaten in twenty-four hours. They harassed us, too, and that second day they opened the cell door and tried to reach in and pull some of the kids out. The kids wouldn't go, and we were trying to close the door while the guards were trying to open it. Part of my arm was hanging outside the bars, and one of the guards slammed down on it with his billy club. Before I could remember about nonviolence I threw the door open and jumped out after him. Right into the arms of five guards.

It was the first really good beating I ever had in my life, a professional job. End to end, up and down, they didn't miss a spot. It didn't really start hurting until about midnight when I tried to touch my face, and I couldn't get my arm up that high. What the hell, if you're willing to die for Freedom, you have to be willing to take a beating. For a couple of days, though, I thought that dying was probably easier.

It was just body pain, though. The Negro has a callus growing on his soul and it's getting harder and harder to hurt him there. That's a simple law of nature. Like a callus on a foot in a shoe that's too tight. The foot is nature's, and that shoe was put on by man. That tight shoe will pinch your foot and make you holler and scream. But sooner or later, if you don't take the shoe off, a callus will form on the foot and begin to wear out the shoe.

It's the same with the Negro in America today. That shoe—the white man's system—has pinched and rubbed and squeezed his soul until it almost destroyed him. But it didn't. And now a callus has formed on his soul, and unless that system is adjusted to fit him, too, that callus is going to wear out that system.

I thought about that for five days in the Birmingham jail while Martin Luther King was waking up America.

III

The night-club audiences were a little more respectful when I came back from Birmingham. After Greenwood there had been hecklers who accused me of demonstrating for publicity. After Birmingham people came backstage to shake my hand and God Bless me and tell me to keep up the good work. White and black. I was surprised. I had thought that being in jail and getting beaten up would cool me off in show business.

I began taking more and more time off, flying to fund-raising benefits, to rallies, to meetings. In May I opened at the hungry i in San Francisco and I wasn't there long before the demonstrations began in Jackson, Mississippi. Medgar Evers was the key man down there, and I called him to ask if I could help. In many ways, Medgar was the man responsible for my being in the civil rights fight. If he hadn't invited me down to Jackson in 1962 I would never have met the old man who lost his wife, and I would never have heard of Clyde Kennard. Medgar asked me to come.

I went to Enrico Banducci, the owner of the hungry i, and I told him I wanted to leave, that my people needed me. A white man, and he had waited all year for my engagement, but he never batted an eye.

"I admire you, Greg. Good luck."

It was that last night in San Francisco, a Saturday night, that I first felt death. Just a funny little feeling in my stomach, a sixth sense that said someone was going to die. I called my lawyer to make sure my will was in order. Then I flew to Chicago to talk to Lil. If I was killed in Jackson, I didn't want my children raised with hate.

She sat on the couch, her eyes wide and tearful, and

I told her what I wanted my children to hear. Just tell them that Daddy was doing right, Lil, tell them it takes a strong soldier to fight when he's outnumbered and the other side has all the dogs, all the fire hoses, all the prods. Don't let them come up with hate, Lil; just show them the beauty in what their Daddy was doing.

I went into the bedroom and I kissed Michele and Lynne, and I kissed Richard Claxton Gregory Junior. He was two and a half months old, and I hadn't had time to know him.

Jim Sanders was waiting for me downstairs, and when I got there I discovered a little switchblade knife in my pocket I had used in my act. I went back upstairs to leave it, and Lil was in the bathroom. Richard Junior had soiled his diaper and he was crying. I picked him up and he stopped crying and smiled. Lil came in and smiled, too.

"That's the first time you ever played with him, Greg."

"There'll be time, honey, time'll come we'll sit and talk father to son."

I kissed him again and promised Lil I'd call as soon as I got to Jackson.

I didn't. The demonstrators put Jim and me up at a Negro minister's house Sunday morning. I figured I'd call later from a pay booth. Jim and I had just gone to sleep when the phone rang. It was Medgar Evers.

"Greg, you better call home."

I got chills. His voice sounded just like Doc Lingle's when the coach came to the movie theater the night Momma died.

"What happened?"

"I don't know. Just call home. Your son's sick."

"No, Medgar, he's not sick. I just held him last night."

"Call home, Greg."

"Why?"

"Just call home, Greg."

"Medgar?"

"I'm sorry, Greg. Your son is dead."

I was numb and I was sick but there was still hope. Until Lil answered the phone, hysterical.

"I'll be right home, honey, I love you very much."

I called Medgar back and told him I was sorry, that I knew what he was doing in Jackson was more important to America than my son dying, but I was leaving. He said he understood. Jim and I left our clothes in Jackson, and flew back to Chicago. It was a very short flight because I didn't know how I was going to face Lil, a woman who had to be mother and father to her children because her husband was a stranger in the house. And I couldn't understand how I had been so sure that I was going to be killed in the heat of battle, only to find out that someone safe and protected had died.

Lil was sitting on the couch when I came in the door. Bob Johnson, editor of *Jet* magazine, was with her. Her eyes came alive for a second when I walked in, then they went dead again. I started toward her and the phone rang. It was a long-distance call from Alabama, collect. I accepted the charges. It was a white woman.

"Mister Gregory?"

"Yes, ma'am."

"I just heard on the radio your son died, and let me tell you it serves you right, I'm real glad that happened, you coming down here where you don't belong and stirring up all . . ."

"I'm glad, too. I had five million dollars' worth of insurance on him."

There was a long silence, and then she said: "I'm sorry, please forgive me."

It was a very long night. Sometimes I got through to Lil for a few minutes, but mostly she just sat still, her hands in her lap, staring at the wall. When she talked her voice was chilly and far away. It was always the same story. She had gone to bed at midnight the night before, soon after I left. At 4 A.M. she woke up to give Richard a feeding. He was the healthiest of all the babies, the best eater. She went back to sleep, knowing that he would wake her at 8 A.M. with his crying, like he always did. But he didn't and she woke up with a start at 9, ran in and picked him up. He was warm, but dead. She ran into the hallway, screaming, and the neighbors called the fire department. They brought an inhalator. One of the doctors at the hospital said he thought it was a kind of overnight pneumonia, a common thing with babies. Later, we found out he was right. Thousands of babies die every year that way.

There were a lot of phone calls that night. All kinds. Most were sympathetic. Some were cruel, and asked for Richard Junior. Some were from ministers because it was suddenly open season on Dick Gregory. It would be a big prestige move to get his son's funeral. One minister taped his five-minute radio show and came by the house just in time to turn the radio on and sit in my living room and listen to himself talk about Dick Gregory's heavy moments. I asked Bob Johnson to get a minister who wouldn't turn the funeral into a carnival, who wouldn't try to take Richard Junior to heaven right in the funeral parlor. He called the Reverend Mack.

The phone rang again. Greenwood. He had a Southern dialect, and for a moment I thought he was a Negro.

"Mister Gregory?"

"Yeah."

"When you coming back down here?"

"First chance I get."

"How come you ain't in Jackson now?"

I heard someone whisper on the other end of the line: "Ask him about his son, ask him about his son." I knew they were white.

"How's your son, Mister Gregory?"

"Just fine, just fine."

"How come you ain't in Jackson now?"

"Didn't feel like going down, you know us niggers are lazy."

"Thought you were in Jackson this morning."

"Oh, man, how can you be so dumb? How could I be in Jackson this morning and talk to you from Chicago tonight? You know, white boy, niggers is scared of airplanes."

"Mister Gregory, tell me some jokes."

"Listen, white boy, us niggers up North are more

sophisticated than you white folks down there. We never work after 11:30 at night. You'll have to call me back during my working hours."

For some reason, when they didn't hear the cry for pity or sympathy or tolerance in my voice, they became ashamed. In their own little way they said they were sorry.

"Good night, Mister Gregory," the voice said softly, and the line went dead.

I went back to Lil. I told her about the phone calls. It upset her, she started to sob.

"Now you understand when I say this thing is bigger than you or me or the kids. When a grown man will call and ask to talk to Richard Junior, you know this thing is bigger than all of us."

She said she understood. Then her mind wandered away again. Michele and Lynne were very quiet, taking care of each other in another room. Lil hadn't told them yet, and I took Michele into the bathroom.

"Michele, honey, where's Richard?"

"Richard's gone, Daddy."

"Gone where?"

"To the hospital."

"When will he be back?"

"He's not coming back, Daddy. You'll have to get another Richard."

"How do you know?"

"I looked at Mommy's face."

It was midnight then, just twenty-four hours since I held him in my arms. I wanted to get back to Jackson, back to the demonstrations, but I had a woman here who was losing her mind. I talked to the minister and told him to go ahead and make the arrangements. I said good night to Bob Johnson, and I put the girls to bed. Now I've got to take care of Lil. And I have to do it fast so I can get back to Jackson with a clear mind.

I walked into our room, and she was lying across the bed, looking at the ceiling. Richard's blanket was clenched to her breast. I decided to take a chance on pulling her out of her shock fast or pushing her deeper in. I knelt next to the bed.

"Lil, can I talk to you?" I touched her and she jerked away.

"Lil, he was my son, too. Can I share it with you, just a little?"

She looked at me and held the look for the first time since I had gotten into town. She grabbed my hand.

"You remember how I thought I was going to be killed in Jackson?"

"Yeah."

"Remember how I came the long way through Chicago to explain not to bring the kids up with hate, and how for the first time I picked Richard Junior up and hugged him and kissed him and played with him?"

"Yes, yes . . ."

"I kissed him and said that Daddy's going to make it a better world for you, not knowing that his world would be over in a few hours. Right?"

"Yes . . ."

"Honey, I left here and went to Mississippi last night knowing it was very easy for me to get killed, thinking I was going to get killed. You know, Lil, if you had been sick, if Richard had been sick and they called me to come out of the South, I never would have come. Right?"

"Yes . . ."

"Remember last year when you had the miscarriage and there was trouble in New Orleans, I just put a blank check in your hand as they were wheeling you out of the house because I had a plane to catch? You know that nothing short of death would have pulled me out of the South today?"

"Yes, Greg, I know that."

"Good, honey, because I wonder if it ever dawned on you that maybe if I hadn't come out of the South today I would have been killed."

"No, it didn't."

"Well, does it make sense to you?"

"Yes."

"You know, Lil, maybe this is the work of God. Maybe to spare my life he took our son's life. Do you believe God could do something like that?"

"Yes."

And then I grabbed her hand hard because I was ready to do the most awful thing I had ever done in my life. I held her hand and looked into her eyes.

"Forget about God. I want you to make the choice."

"What do you mean, Greg?"

"You have the decision now, Lil. Forget about God. If you had the decision to make this morning that I was to be killed in Mississippi, and the only way you could spare my life was to take Richard's, which one of us would you have taken?"

I knelt there and I looked at a woman's face that was so distorted it wasn't even human, a face with two holes for eyes that were filled with hate for me. She jerked and twisted and I jumped up and pinned her down on the bed and I screamed at her.

"Forget about God. It's your decision, you make the decision, me or Richard Junior, me or Richard Junior. . . ."

And she twisted and rolled and tried to get free and screamed and kicked, and then suddenly she went limp. For the first time her eyes were clear, and her body relaxed and the tears rolled freely down her cheeks.

"Richard Junior . . ." she said.

After the funeral, Jim Sanders and I went back to Jackson. All the way down I wondered if I had a right to shock a woman out of crying, out of a grief a mother has to feel when her only son dies in the same room. And because Lil had pulled out of it so strongly, and because I was now away from it all, I think I went into shock myself, realizing for the first time what had happened. Over and over again I thought about that feeling of death I had, and how it was a little baby, safe and sound, not a soldier on the battle line, who had died. Then we were in Mississippi again.

We didn't stay long this time. There was a strangeness

in the air, the demonstrations weren't going well. Kids were coming to demonstrate and they were being sent back to get notes from their parents. I saw two young Negroes, one a soldier, walking on the streets and I asked them why they weren't demonstrating. The soldier said because he was in the Army. Sure, I told him, the same Army that will send you all over the world to guarantee a foreigner his rights. His friend said he wasn't demonstrating because he was too violent. That's right, I told him, and when the doors of segregation get kicked down and they're ready to hire their first Negro detective are you going to refuse the job because you're too violent? They both said they'd demonstrate.

Lena Horne came down to speak, and that did a lot of good for the people, to hear someone they idolized say: "I'm with you." This is especially important in an area where the church is afraid to wake up and carry the ball.

I talked to Medgar Evers, told him that something bad was going to happen in Jackson, things seemed so wrong. But I didn't know what it was, and somehow there didn't seem to be anything I could do here. I remember Medgar cried—I guess he felt it, too. I told him I was sorry to be leaving again, but he knew that anytime he called me I would come back. Anytime. He said he knew.

We went back to San Francisco, started working again at the hungry i. I apologized to Enrico Banducci for having left in the middle of an engagement, but I told him that as long as I stayed hot as a comic I'd work for him every year.

I don't know if my mind was really on my work those first two days at the hungry i, thinking about Lil, about Medgar, about Richard Junior. Somehow I still couldn't understand that feeling I had a week before in San Francisco about death, about someone being killed. I was so sure it would be me, and then it turned out to be a little baby born in one of the world's best baby hospitals, born into money and love and care. It didn't make sense.

And, of course, it didn't. The second night back at the hungry i, Billy Daniels drove over from a singing engagement in Berkeley to tell me that Medgar Evers had been murdered.

IV

When we walked behind the body of Medgar Evers through the streets of Jackson the line stretched so far back it looked like ants in a parade, old folks, young folks, black and light and white folks, nappy hair and pressed hair and blow hair, Thom McAn and Buster Brown and barefoot, they walked and they walked. It looked like we had enough folks to march on God that day. We turned a corner and the same white policemen who had fought Medgar so hard were directing traffic at his funeral procession. They were holding up their white gloves, telling Whitey in his car he'd have to stop for Medgar Evers now. And Whitey sat in his car and watched the funeral go by, the same Whitey who didn't say a word when a man was fighting for right and truth and justice, who didn't open his mouth when that man was shot in the back in front of his house. And Whitey in his car had to be scared that day when he saw that procession go by, scared to realize that when you shoot right and truth and justice down, more right and truth and justice will rise up.

It was hot that day, more than 100 degrees. I was wet from the cuffs of my pants to the lapels on my jacket, hot and wet inside my shoes. When I pulled out my handkerchief and squeezed it, water ran down my hand.

The press was there that day, and I remember the way everybody gasped a little when a photographer from *Life* magazine almost stood on Medgar's coffin to get a picture of Mrs. Evers. I gasped, too, but when I saw that picture, that beautiful picture of a single tear running down Mrs. Evers' face, I knew that photographer could have stood inside that coffin and it would have been all right.

Jim Sanders and I went back to San Francisco and the hungry i that night. Jim asked me how I could be funny that night. I told him that when a man sells his talents he's a prostitute, and when you're a prostitute you lay like the customer wants you to lay.

I was funny that night.

V

It was like being in the forest in the daytime when the sun is shining and everybody's having picnics and laughing and playing ball, and then suddenly it's night and you're alone. You're running through the pitch-black cold, running away from something that's whipping down on your head and shoulders, maybe running in the wrong direction, and your legs hurt and your stomach hurts and it starts to rain, hard and cold, and finally you can't run any more and you lay down and say: "All right, catch me." And suddenly the rain quits and the sun comes out and you see you've been running away from the branches of trees that look so friendly and beautiful in the sunshine again. The birds start singing and the rabbits start running. You just cock your hand under your head and lie there, and you can't hold back that smirky smile when a little squirrel comes over and licks your cheek and a little bird flies down on your chest. And you ask yourself. "What was I so afraid of a few minutes ago?" And then suddenly it's pitch-black cold again, and you're running again and you know the answer. That was the summer of 1963.

The summer began in St. Louis, a week after Medgar Evers' funeral. The AAU was holding its national track and field championships, and selecting a team to compete against the Russian team in Moscow. I asked the Negro athletes to boycott the Moscow meet. I told them I'd rather see this country embarrassed than destroyed. They didn't understand.

I talked to them, I negotiated with them, I stood on street corners and passed out handbills. I screamed at them. Damn you, listen. An American Negro can go to Moscow and run in an integrated track meet on enemy territory, but he can't run in an integrated track meet in parts of his own home country. You can bust this thing if you want to. It's one thing to defend your country in a track meet, that's fine, but you have a chance to save your country.

But they were young. They didn't want to embarrass their country, to bring this thing into the open, to push this thing out on an international level. They couldn't seem to understand that if Khrushchev came to this country with his Russian track team and demanded that the meet be held in New Orleans he would beat us because no Negroes could compete. I flew back from the track meet in St. Louis disgusted and downhearted. Those athletes could have saved it right there. They would have embarrassed this country so bad it would have cleaned house. But they didn't and so this country just swept a little more filth under the rug, and didn't look to see that the other end was on fire.

After the failure in St. Louis, I took Lil and the kids to Honolulu for a vacation. Over there you can think, you can try to seek wisdom, you can reach out and touch nature. I went to rest and I ended up doing a couple of benefit performances and radio shows. They told me there was very little racial prejudice in Hawaii. Like a woman is just a little bit pregnant.

When we came back to Chicago there was a letter waiting for me that brought tears to my eyes. I had made *Who's Who in America.*

That's why so many people are willing to lay down their lives to save this great country from the cancer of hate that is destroying it. Where else in the world could a Negro, born and raised on relief, make *Who's Who?* In 1952 I was a welfare case, and in 1963 I was on a list of famous men. In America, with all of its evils and faults, you can still reach through the forest and see the sun. But we don't know yet whether that sun is rising or setting for our country.

I lay on a couch in our living room and I read and I reread that letter from *Who's Who* and I cried and I was thrilled and I felt strong. I turned on the radio and heard that they were demonstrating in Chicago for better schools, and that they had arrested some people. I called James, and Lil and I got dressed and went downtown.

In Chicago they arrested us for disorderly conduct. In Birmingham, in Jackson, anywhere in the South I've been arrested, it's been for parading without a permit. In my own town—in the North—I found less dignity and less truth than I found in Mississippi. In the South we were treated as demonstrators—as bad as that might be —and kept together with other demonstrators. In Chicago we were treated as convicts. Our clothes were pulled off, our belongings were taken away. We might have had a very bad time in prison if the authorities were in control, but the convicts ran that prison and they were sympathetic. I guess they had never seen people brought into the House of Correction who refused to post bond, and who were being jailed for right.

It leaves a bitter taste in your mouth to see Negro policemen arresting Negro and white civil rights demonstrators in the North. But it makes you sick to the stomach to see what really goes on in these Northern jails. I had never been with convicts before. I couldn't believe that they ran the prison, that if you wanted cigarettes or a clean shirt or a telephone call to the outside you just had to go through one of the convict leaders. I think you could have gotten more pure heroin in that Chicago jail than on a South Side street. Any prisoner who didn't know how to lie and cheat and steal and threaten before he went to jail, sure learned fast there. Many of them carried knives. And they'd fight like dogs over their women —the pretty, younger homosexuals.

We had some trouble in jail—me, James, and a white demonstrator. First they tried to make the white boy work in the junkyard. So James and I refused to go to our clerical jobs. We hadn't been sentenced yet, and so legally we didn't have to work off our sentences. We were thrown in solitary confinement.

The convict leader was a Southern Negro who had been a pimp, robber, dope pusher, mugger. He had done a lot of reading, because he had spent most of his life in jail; in a year, out a year, in again. He told me he was doing a life sentence on the installment plan. He came to see me in solitary and he said he was impressed with the beauty and truth of the movement. He said he might not be in jail if there were equal rights. Then he said he'd get me out of solitary. I just thanked him. I didn't believe he could.

I had a lot to learn about prisons. That evening, after dinner, the convict leader went right up to the chief security officer.

"Eat your last can of sauerkraut, Polack, because one of us has to die unless Mister Gregory and his people get out of solitary."

We were taken out of solitary.

It was the trial that really bothered me. It was supposed to be a short bench trial and it lasted all day. It was the first time I had ever been on trial in the North, and the first time the police ever lied on me.

I guess in the South they don't have to. The cops call you nigger, the judge calls you nigger, and everybody knows you're going to get time. But up North, where they can't come out and call you nigger, they have to go through the motions of a fair trial.

They lied from the beginning of that trial to the end. I cried. One of the Chicago policemen accused Jim Sanders of talking back to him and raising his hand to him. Another swore that they had made no arrests until I showed up and the crowd at the demonstration site got out of hand. It was brought out in the trial that the complaint against me had never been signed. Eleven days in prison and the complaint hadn't been signed. The judge adjourned the trial, and then he refused to rule on the case. And then he turned me loose, back to Mayor Richard J. Daley's corrupt Chicago—Massa Daley's plantation, as us slaves call it.

Then I went out to Los Angeles for a night-club engagement, but I flew back East for one day, the day that turned that summer into a beautiful thing, that turned the darkness of the forest into daylight. The day we marched on Washington.

That was a glory day. For the first time in history the policy wheel closed down in Washington, and one of the classiest, richest whores in the country asked me to lend her thirty dollars. She said she wanted to go to Washington with clean money.

Whitey expected violence and he had a picnic on his hands. Couldn't understand how a people with a 300-year-old gripe could gather together in one place without breaking heads. Wars have started over weekend border disputes. Oh, baby, we came with brand-new shoes and wigs and Sunday clothes because it was the first time *all* of us—not just Mister Nobel Prize Winner or Mister Big Entertainer—were ever invited somewhere. I brought Lil and the kids. I didn't want them to miss a part of the twentieth century.

When we got off the plane I was so nervous and proud I rushed right to the hotel and changed suits—I didn't want to wear a wrinkled one. Ossie Davis had asked me to help him emcee the television part of the show, but I turned him down. There was some bad feeling among whites toward me for demonstrating and I didn't want to bug anyone in their living room that day, I didn't want the least little thing to mar this beautiful day. And you can believe I wanted to stand up before that audience.

We watched the people walking through the streets. A rabbi with a sign written in Hebrew, and just from the expression on his face you knew that sign said something nice. Saw a man bump into another man and they both said, "Excuse me." Martin Luther King had told us not to put mayonnaise on our chicken because he didn't want anyone passing out, and we didn't put mayonnaise on our chicken. And we put those chicken bones in our pockets.

Oh, baby, to stand on the top of the Lincoln Memorial and look down, it was like everyone in the world was standing there, smiling in the sunshine and singing. Saw Negroes and whites in their best clothes, with their best manners, on their best behavior. And the Negroes, people that Whitey says don't qualify for first-class citizenship, demonstrated to the world that day that we're more first-class than a lot of whites. And Bayard Rustin, the man who engineered that March. When will Whitey realize that men like Rustin can help him solve his world problems?

They came over to me and asked me to say a few words. I told them I didn't want to. They insisted. I was really happy they did. I said a few humorous words, then went to sit on the grass with my family.

The climax of that beautiful day was Martin Luther King's speech, "I Have a Dream." Never have so many people cried, whether they wanted to or not. When it was all over I just sat there because I didn't know which way to go. Thought of a million and one things, oh, how my mind wandered that glorious day. That day I felt like the Negro had been given his equal rights.

I felt that way right into September, right into the Sunday morning when the forest turned pitch-black cold again. Someone threw a bomb in a Negro church in Birmingham. Four kids were dead.

VI

Another funeral. It wasn't like Medgar Evers' funeral. This one was by invitation only. But they came anyway, the poor, the raggedy, the verb-buster. Outside the church I saw an old Negro woman in torn tennis shoes holding onto an old Negro man who had a wine bottle in his pocket. I was glad when the television cameras took pictures of that old couple. Those kids died for *all* Negroes, not just those who were invited.

But I guess the greatest lesson of that Birmingham bombing was for the Negro who thought that civil rights didn't pertain to him—the principal, the teacher, the doctor, the preacher, the lawyer. Those were his kids in that church, and whether he wanted to demonstrate or not, whether he thought we were going too fast or not, he found out that as long as your skin is black . . .

Three of the children lay inside the church. I talked to one of the mothers. Both of her daughters were in the bombing. One daughter got glass in her eyes, and the mother spent five hours in a hospital operating room waiting to find out if she would ever see again. A few minutes after she learned that one daughter would be not blind for life, she learned that her other daughter was dead.

After a while, Lil and I walked over to the church that had been bombed. We saw a strange and terrible thing. All the windows but one had been completely blown out. The stained glass window of Christ was almost intact. Only Christ's eyes and the top of His head were blown out. And it frightened me because I wondered what it meant.

Christ with no eyes. The blind leading the blind? Christ with no mind.

We left and I told Lil that she had seen a great work of art because it had taken a hundred years of hate and violence to produce an artist capable of creating that picture. But it wasn't the only frightening symbol I saw in Birmingham that day.

I saw a state policeman with a tommy gun cradled in his arm, a smile on his face, leaning against a mailbox across the street from the church. The mailbox was painted red, white, and blue.

VII

A scared Negro is one thing. A mad Negro is something
else. I had always gone down South scared. But in September, when I went down to Selma, Alabama, Whitey
had a mad Negro on his hands.

Those brave, beautiful kids from SNCC had started
their big voter registration drive in Selma, and had asked
me to help them. I was too sick to travel, but I didn't
want to let them down. I sent Lillian in my place. She
was pregnant again. We didn't know it at the time, but
she was carrying twin girls. Lillian was in jail a week
before I was able to get to Selma.

It was a Friday night. I talked to Lillian through a
jailhouse window, and she said everything was all right.
Then I went to speak at a rally. I walked through a dep-
utized posse of 200 rednecks, into a church that had
been tear-gassed a few days before. I got up on stage in
front of a crowd of scared Negroes. They needed some
courage. Courage to go out and buck the system, courage to let their children demonstrate, courage to stand
up and be counted in a town where the front row of
their church was filled that night with policemen pretending to be newspaper reporters and taking notes. I di-
rected my speech at those cops in the front row. I was
mad. I told that audience how surprised I was to see a
dumb Southern cop who knew how to write. The crowd
was nervous. They had never heard such talk in front of
a white man before.

*It always amazes me to see how the Southern white
folks will knock themselves out, pose as all kinds of
things to slip into a Negro meeting, and we haven't gotten around to wanting to slip into a Ku Klux Klan meet-
ting. I think that speaks for itself. The whole world*

wants to slip in and be around right and good and Godliness, but only fools want to be around filth.

They looked at each other and giggled nervously, but they sat up a little straighter.

A Southern white man. Only thing he has to be able to identify with is a drinking fountain, a toilet, and the right to call me nigger.

They liked that. A few people clapped, and somebody yelled: "You tell 'em, brother."

Every white man in America knows we are Americans, knows we are Negroes, and some of them know us by our names. So when he calls us a nigger, he's calling us something we are not, something that exists only in his mind. So if nigger exists only in his mind, who's the nigger?

They laughed and they clapped.

Now let's take it one step further. This is a Bible here. We know it's a book. Now if I sat here and called it a bicycle, I have called it something it is not. So where does the bicycle exist? In my mind. I'm the sick one, right?

And they were cheering now, and screaming and laughing and the white cops up front looked pale. The crowd wasn't afraid of them.

I talked for about an hour that Friday night. I told them how important it was for them to get out and support the voter registration drive on Monday. If they registered, they could vote, and if they voted the politicians would represent their interests, too.

Saturday, Lillian came out of jail, and Saturday night I went back to the church to speak again. Before I began, I asked the audience to sing, "Were You There When They Crucified the Lord?" Then I started, and I wasn't mad any more, and I laid it down to them.

It's amazing how we come to this church every Sunday and cry over the crucifixion of Christ, and we don't cry over these things that are going on around and among us. If He was here now and saw these things, He would cry. And He would take those nails again. For us. For this problem.

It just so happened that in His day and time, religion was the big problem. Today, it is color.

What do you think would happen to Christ tonight if He arrived in this town a black man and wanted to register to vote on Monday? What do you think would happen? Would you be there? You would? Then how come you're not out there with these kids, because He said that whatever happens to the least, happens to us all . . .

Let's analyze the situation.

We're not saying, "Let's go downtown and take over City Hall."

We're not saying, "Let's stand on the rooftops and throw bricks at the white folks."

We're not saying, "Let's get some butcher knives and some guns and make them pay for what they've done."

We're talking to the white man, and this is what we're saying.

We're saying, "We want what you said belongs to us. You have a constitution. I'm a black man, and you make me sit down in a black school and take a test on the United States Constitution, a constitution that hasn't worked for anyone but you. And you expect me to learn it from front to back. So I learned it.

"You made me stand up as a little kid and sing 'God Bless America,' and 'America the Beautiful,' and all those songs the white kids were singing. I Pledge Allegiance to the Flag. That's all I'm asking you for today."

Something important happened in 1963, and the sooner we wake up and realize it, the better off this whole world is going to be. Because for some reason God has put in your hands the salvation of not just America—this thing is bigger than just this country—but the salvation of the whole world. . . .

The Negro in America has the highest standard of living, the highest educational standard, the highest medical standard of any black man the world over and of most white men outside America. And yet there are backward countries getting more respect from this American white man than you people could ever command. Do you know why?

It's because we grinned when he wanted us to grin. We cried when he wanted us to cry. We've spent money when he wanted us to spend money. And we've done without when he said do without.

He owns all the missiles in the world, and when he talks to you about owning a switchblade you become ashamed.

He started all the wars, and when he talks to you about cutting somebody on Saturday night you become ashamed.

He makes me feel small. He calls me everything on the job but my name, so I'm aggravated before I get home.

Then he tells me about my education. Well, if it takes education his-style to produce a clown that would throw dynamite in a church, I hope we never get that.

I have a newspaper and I wish I brought it tonight. It embarrasses me just to look at it. It's a newspaper from 1848, a New Orleans newspaper.

On the back page are ads offering rewards for the return of runaway slaves. Can you believe in 1848 we were running away, rebelling, and we didn't have any place to run to? 1848. Slaves were running away.

Can you imagine what this old Negro had to go through? Can you imagine the day a Negro woman went to a black man and said: "Honey, I'm pregnant," and both of them fell on their knees and prayed that their baby would be born deformed? Can you imagine what this Negro went through, hoping his baby is born crippled?

Because if he was born crippled, he would have less chance of being a slave and more chance of having freedom.

Think about that. Think about the woman you love coming to you and saying she's pregnant with your baby and you both pray the baby is born crippled.

This is what the slaves went through. And a hundred years later, we have parallels.

A hundred years later and you people are worrying about your kids being in jail overnight, being in jail because they demonstrated for freedom. So many parents who don't even know where their kids are, for the first time they'll know where their kids are twenty-four hours a day. In jail. And know that they're there for a good cause and a good reason.

How many mothers let their sons play football, and all he can get from that is a chance to help his team win a victory. A victory that will be forgotten tomorrow. So can't you let your son fight for freedom, something that the whole world will profit from, forever?

Sometimes I wonder how much this system has corrupted us. Sometimes I wonder when we will wake up to see that the day is over when we can say: "I'm not involved."

Those four kids who were killed in that church in Birmingham, they weren't demonstrating.

You don't have to participate. Just be black. Or be white, and for our cause. When the bomb is thrown, somebody has to die.

And do you know that 50 per cent of the killings are our fault? That's right. We let this white man go crazy on us, instead of straightening him out when we should have.

Each one of us scratched our heads five years too long.

Sure, tomming was good once upon a time. That's how we got here. The old folks knew that was the only way they could raise you. What we call Uncle Tomism today was nothing but finesse and tact then. The old folks had to scratch their heads and grin their ways into a white man's heart. A white man who wouldn't accept them any other way.

But at what point do we stop tomming?

A Negro is better off going to a foreign country fighting for America than he is coming to the South fighting for the Negro cause. When he's in a foreign country, fighting to give those people rights he doesn't even get,

*the whole of America is behind him. When he comes
down here, there are only a few behind him.*

*So it's coming down to this. You have to commit.
You're going through the same thing today that the folks
went through when the Lord was crucified.*

"Who else is with Christ?" the Romans asked.

*And everybody just stood there. And prayed silently.
And they went back and said: "I prayed."*

No, sister, I didn't even see your lips move.

*Were you there when they crucified the Lord? It's a
nice song to sing. But this time, you have an opportunity
to be there.*

*Sure would be a heck of a thing, twenty, thirty years
from now when they're singing a song about these days,
and your grand-kids and great-grand-kids can stand up
and say: "Yeah, baby, he was there, my grandfather was
there."*

*And when they ask you, you can nod your head and
say: "Yeah, I was there."*

*I'd like to tell you a story before I leave. I talked to
the father of one of the kids who died in that church in
Birmingham. He said to me: "You know, Gregory, my
daughter begged me to let her demonstrate, and I told
her no. I told her she was too young. And she looked at
me, and she said: 'Then you do it, Daddy.' "* . . .

*And that's what that man will have to live with for
the rest of his life. Because if Birmingham had had
enough Negroes behind them, there wouldn't have been
a bombing. . . .*

*These kids here in Selma aren't doing anything just for
themselves. There's nothing selfish about what they're
doing here. Freedom will run all over this town. But you
have to get behind them. Because there are too many
white folks in front of them.*

Get behind your kids in this town.

Good-by and God Bless You and Good Night.

The next morning Lil and I went home. It's hard to
say good-by to people in the South, people you're leaving behind on the battle line. They have that look in

their eyes, thanks a million, please don't go. They were singing "We Shall Overcome," as we drove out of Selma, and somehow we could still hear them on the plane back to Chicago.

That Sunday we took the kids to a drive-in movie. Michele and Lynne sat in the back of the car, one on each side of Lil. On the way, Michele pointed out the window.

"What's that, Mommy?"

"That's a filling station, Michele, it sells gasoline. Daddy's car runs on gasoline, all cars run on gasoline. Look over there, Michele, across the street. That's another filling station. You see, honey, there are different kinds of gas, there's Shell, and over there, that's Standard, and now, look over there. . . ."

I'm driving with tears in my eyes. Here's a woman who just spent eight days in jail, and she's able to sit back there, so patient and kind, and tell her kids about the different kinds of gasoline. I wish I had that kind of beauty. I wish the world was that free from malice and hate.

VIII

They burst into my hotel room, a dozen of them, laughing and screaming and singing, and for a moment all I saw were the flickering flames the first one was carrying in his hands. I jumped up and my stomach turned over and then I was angry because they had scared me, and then I cried. It was a cake with candles. It was my first birthday party. I was thirty-one.

Jim Sanders was there, and his new wife, Jackie, and my managers and agents and writers and some of the other performers from the night club. We drank and we talked and they didn't believe this was my first real party. And I told them about Richard, the kid I once knew in St. Louis who used to buy himself a Twinkie Cupcake and steal a little pink candle and pretend he was having a party.

Oh, Momma, I wish you could see your little Richard now. He's all right. I didn't lie to you, Momma, about people buying me birthday presents, about people inviting me over to their houses. It's true now, so it's no lie any more. And you know, Momma, that old lady who saw a star in the middle of my forehead, she was right. We thought I was going to be a great athlete, and we were wrong, and I thought I was going to be a great entertainer, and that wasn't it, either. I'm going to be an American citizen. First-class.

Hot damn, we're going to bust this thing. I feel it when I stand in front of a crowd of people hungry for freedom, and I feel it when we march down a street for our rights. Hot water seeping up into a cold body, that dry taste in my mouth. The monster. But it's not content to beat some mother's son in a foot race any more, and it's not satisfied to make people laugh and love me. Now it wants some respect and dignity, and it wants freedom. It's willing to die for freedom.

It's getting stronger every day. It would frighten you, Momma. But now it has truth and justice and the Constitution of the greatest country in the world on its side.

It's not just a Negro monster. I saw it in a Northern white boy who marched with us for freedom through the snow in Georgia. He had no soles on his shoes, and his feet were blue and he never said a word. I asked him why he didn't go home and take that big engineering job he had been offered. He said that there would be nothing to build on unless every American citizen got his rights first.

When I saw him, Momma, I laughed at every Northern liberal who ever said: "Slow down, you people, don't alienate your friends." Yeah, baby, were you there when they crucified the Lord? Or were you just singing?

Yeah, that monster's growing stronger, Momma, I saw it in New York where we marched against school segregation, Northern-style, marched to give little black kids a chance for a better education and college and good jobs. And a chance for little white kids to sit with us and know us and learn to love and hate us as individuals, not just fear and hate us as a color like their parents do.

I saw it in Chester, Pennsylvania, with Stanley Branche where we marched for equal opportunities, a chance to be ordinary if we wanted, to be great if we could. Just a chance to be Americans.

I saw it in Atlanta where we marched against segregation in restaurants. I was in my first sit-in there, and I did my first official negotiating. I learned that when honesty sits around a conference table, black men and white men can understand and feel each other's problems, and help each other.

I saw the monster in Mississippi where we marched for voter registration, so a Negro can cast his ballot for the government he lives under and supports with his tax money, and dies for in wars.

I saw it in San Francisco where white doctors and lawyers marched on the lines with us and went to jail with us and showed the world that this isn't a revolution of black against white, this is a revolution of right against wrong. And right has never lost.

This is a revolution. It started long before I came into it, and I may die before it's over, but we'll bust this thing and cut out this cancer. America will be as strong and beautiful as it should be, for black folks and white folks. We'll all be free then, free from a system that makes a man less than a man, that teaches hate and fear and ignorance.

You didn't die a slave for nothing, Momma. You brought us up. You and all those Negro mothers who gave their kids the strength to go on, to take that thimble to the well while the whites were taking buckets. Those of us who weren't destroyed got stronger, got calluses on our souls. And now we're ready to change a system, a system where a white man can destroy a black man with a single word. Nigger.

When we're through, Momma, there won't be any niggers any more.